The Happiness Journal

Your daily inspirational sips toward reaching happiness

Viet Hung

Dedication

This book is for anyone who is burdened by worries, fears, or insecure feelings that may be blocking their path toward happiness. I hope my experiences during the past twenty years, as both a professional and an entrepreneur will bring you inspiration and useful suggestions.

You can use these thoughts to find your own direction and live a noble, confident, and fulfilling life to the fullest extent - **a happy life**.

Editorial reviews

The Happiness Journal is designed to be savored in small doses. It's a simple book that will leave readers feeling refreshed and uplifted with every "sip." — **Blueink Review**

Incisive observations on happiness drawn from Eastern philosophy. — **Kirkus Reviews**

Author Viet Hung's perspective as a Vietnamese businessman adds a unique spin to THE HAPPINESS JOURNAL, and his earnest and easy to engage with writing style and use of QR codes to expand the impact of the book is both inventive and effective. — **Indie Reader**

An engaging collection of astute observations. The cumulative effect is feeling a sense of peace and hope - if not outright happiness than a real sense of potential for appreciating what life has to offer, and avoiding those things that bring it down, so the book is successful in its intent. Anyone seeking advice and comfort, whether for currently arising challenges or a general sense of longing for a more peaceful path, will benefit from Hung's well-considered, sensible, and stimulating selections. — **Self-Publishing Review**

A very informative book that would guide us towards an ultimate success."The Happiness Journal" by Viet Hung is definitely the most reliable source of warding off all the burdens of a depressed and worried mind. It acts like a tranquilizer and heals the mind more than a prescribed dose of a tranquilizer might ever do. The book in itself is a well-established rehabilitation center, it shows us the way towards a life full of all the meanings that we wouldn't be able to explore otherwise.
— **Reedsy Discovery**

Content

Foreword 9
PART 1 - SENSING HAPPINESS 13
    Big vs. small 15
    Facing your fears 16
    Whose fault is it? 20
    Don't lose faith in this world 22
    1000 24
    Victim mentality is a universal issue 26
    Positive thinking vs. negative thinking 28
    Who can bother me? 30
    With reading comes miracles 32
    "The truth will set you free…" 34
    I certainly call this happiness 35
    Happy Thanksgiving 2014 37
    Dealing with sadness 39
    What lies behind difficulties 41
    Giving or receiving? 43
    Live and die 45
    The little me 46
    Learn and observe from nature 47
    Alone 48
    Mosquito bite 49
    Stillness 51
    The nose 53
    The fish and the turtle 54
    A cloud has no legs 56
    Peace comes from living by a code of ethics 58
    Is there one person to trust and love me? 60
    "What did I do wrong for more than half of my life?" 61
    Alleviate suffering 62
    A dog and a piece of bone 63
    Unconditional love 64
    Joyfulness comes from what we do, not necessarily from the outcome of it 65
    Yen Tu challenge 66
    Life is a school without a graduation ceremony 74
    Time…tick, tock! 76
    Impermanence 78
    You can rely on yourself! 80
    Reward yourself with peace 81
    United with nature! 83
    Alone, but not lonely 84
PART 2: HAPPINESS IN THE WORKPLACE 85
    Hell or heaven? 87
    The piece of log and the Buddha statue 89
    Where does self-confidence come from? 91
    What do you need to deliver inspirational public talks? 93
    Peaceful mind vs. passionate pursuit 94
    Changing fate and creating luck 97
    Five qualities to build your success and more importantly your

happiness	100
The word "family"	108
Are you proud of what you are doing?	110
Higher positions, attachments, greed, and how to deal with it all	112
A question about respect	116
An ideally happy job	118
Becoming a great manager	122
What makes a band so powerful?	125
Five things I learned from my entrepreneurial journey	127
PART 3: SEEKING YOUR OWN TRUTHFUL HAPPINESS	137
Two questions for your life	139
What is happiness?	142
Things change, anyway	145
Two wolves	146
Maintain good health	148
How to gain self-confidence	152
Where to seek happiness	156
The barrier to happiness…	159
Accumulating peace	160
The wheel of life	161
Tears of happiness	163
Happiness starts with its definition	167
Necessary space for the mind	169
To a peaceful 2019!	171
Most of us fail in our search for happiness…but we can succeed	174
Preparing for our next life	177
A quiet lake	178
Hell and freedom	179
Freedom lies directly ahead	180
Beautiful moments	181
The barrier of detachment	182
"The myth is stronger than the truth…"	187
The marks waves leave	189
THE LAST FEW WORDS	193
About the author	197

Foreword

Life is really…well, life. You plan in order to get one thing done, but then usually something different happens.

I have started my very first book project, called ***The Happiness Journey 1.0***, a few years ago. However, at the moment it's only about 80% of completion of the manuscript. It turned out that my very first book published is another one. That is the very one you're holding in your hands now. It is a gift I want to give to my family and my friends and to anyone I am able to meet and possibly inspire.

This book is a collection of blog posts I've written over the past ten years. After having assembled the content, I realized that it's worth sharing the happy and meaningful moments I've been lucky enough to experience. These short articles reflect my thoughts and feelings throughout my own ongoing journey to happiness. I hope my ideas can be an ample source of inspiration and encouragement for you to be able to live a happy, fulfilled, and well-rounded life, a life full of energy like what I have had (at least, so far).

I seriously started writing a blog in 2009. Since then, I've kept writing and following my own senses, feelings, and thoughts without thinking too much about who would read my posts. Now that I've read through all of my posts again, I'm thrilled to see that the core values I chose to adopt at the beginning of my journey are still fresh and still hold true ten years later. They have helped bring many happy moments and luck into my life!

My core values came into being alongside two important milestones in my life. First, I started my own company, KMS Technology Vietnam, where I was the co-founder and managing director. Second, my wife and I welcomed my little lovely daughter into our lives in August of 2009. Both of these events were wonderful gifts, yet they were also the two biggest challenges of my life. And they were infinite sources of inspiration for me to live better in this world.

Through my writings, I hope to fulfill one and only one wish: to inspire everyone to have a positive, well-rounded, peaceful, meaningful, fulfilled, energetic, and intense life. That's the kind of life I believe in. It's a life that is realistic and achievable, one that's worth living in the midst of so many challenges, difficulties, unexpected events, and burdens that each of us has to deal with every day.

Another note worth sharing is that I'm not native English speaker. Much of the content of this book has been translated from my Vietnamese blog posts, and I translated the content myself. I am using very simple English. I also think speaking with an authentic voice is important. I hope reading my book will feel like I am having a direct conversation with you, telling you stories about my life and my happiness.

I am a big fan of a book called *Mindfulness in Plain English* — it's a great book for anyone who wants to meditate. From that book, I learned that if you can't use simple and plain language to explain what you know, you fail. Because you may not have enough an in-depth understanding of things to explain. And so, I've challenged myself to use simple vocabulary and phrasing throughout this book.

And a final note: as you're reading this book, you can read the articles in any sequence. Each of the articles is like a thoughtful sip of coffee, and each has its own meaning to contemplate.
Enjoy reading!

The Happiness Journal

PART 1: SENSING HAPPINESS

We're born, we grow up, we get old, and we ultimately depart from this life. That's a harsh and inevitable yet natural process. Interestingly, some questions accompany us throughout the course of our lives:
- Are we living, or just existing?
- Are we living for ourselves and being ourselves, or are we just living a dependent life?
- With each moment that passes by, what can we learn from it?
- What is the meaning that this life brings to us?

The Happiness Journal

Big vs. small

On an early Saturday morning in Cu Chi, a Catholic nun opened her gate for me, welcoming me into a house that was home to more than 50 orphans and differently abled children. I stood in front of her and was kind of shocked. Though she was only as tall as my shoulder, I felt like I was the one who was too small, like I was a child myself. How was that possible when she was a skinny, short woman with a soft voice? (Although she did have many, many big and kind smiles.) I quickly found out the answer, and it was an answer rooted in human kindness. It was also a deep lesson for me. The answer was simply "**her heart.**"

I have a little daughter of my own, and everyone in my house has to run around constantly in order to raise and care for her. Yet this nun was raising more than 50 children coming from difficult circumstances who had no blood relationship with her. In addition, many of them were differently abled. That nun and all of her sister nuns in the house had completely dedicated their hearts and souls, energy and money, sweat and tears, laughter and sorrows into each and every minute to keep the house warm and welcoming for those children.

That nun had such a great big heart and mind! Her giant heart was making me felt tiny as I stood in front of her. We are not big or small because of our physical body. No! We can only be as big as our heart and our kindness.

Facing your fears

I once received a long email from a stranger who shared with me his difficulties, his fears, and a lot of his worries. He wrote the email without even a hope that I would read it, but I did, and I was glad I did. Most of us (including myself) face our fears every day as we live our lives. Below is what I wrote back to him.

Hi, bro!

Everyone has problems like yours. Everyone has a lot of fears: a fear of not being successful, a fear of looking bad in front of others, a fear of getting sick. Sometimes we just have fears for no known reasons. I think the problem itself is not fear because everyone has fears. (Including me!) Essentially, the question is, how do you deal with your fears?

The simplest answer is to do something to improve the situation instead of procrastinating — that just makes things worse. I used to have a lot more fears and worries than I do now. I used to worry about my health, my finances, my safety, and the safety of my family. I even used to worry about the individual futures of other people! (Which are of course harder to directly impact.) But now I worry less and less.

Whether you worry less or more depends on the thoughts, actions, and statements you keep cultivating in the now. Procrastinating and not doing anything to improve your current situation is like you're sending your burdens into a saving account. With each passing day, you add more burdens, creating interest that adds to the base of worries that is already there. As a result, you become more exhausted and more insecure, and the burdens keep piling up. That's a disappointingly infinite loop, right?

I'm guessing you feel much better now that you've shared everything with me through your writing. You're really good at one important thing: you've admitted your failures. Knowing and accepting your problems is like you've already solved 50% of your problems. Now you know exactly what your real burdens are!

The first step is to take your burdens off your shoulders and directly face them. You should not carry them on your shoulders and at the same time try to run away from them. In an objective reality, there are no labels of "failure" or "success," because if we never fail, how can we know success? Those are just concepts and labels we stick onto things. They are not overly important.

The more important thing is this: what can you learn from failures or successes? Remember, you don't need to label them for any reason. This process of learning and observing what is happening to you goes on nonstop throughout your lifetime. Right now, you're suffering because your mind is drowning in a negative mental state of being burdened, of being tired, of being disappointed. Here's an idea for how to deal with those thoughts: you can write them down on toilet paper and flush them down the toilet. It is a simple way for your mind to declare "Goodbye!" to those negative feelings. After you've done that, then you can start working on bringing yourself out of those burdensome and negative states of mind.

Here's another thing you can do: buy an item from Nike (a hat, a T-shirt, a pair of shoes). Why? Because Nike has a great slogan that says "JUST DO IT." You need to learn that slogan by heart. Do something! Do anything that can help you improve your situation instead of procrastinating and nurturing more and more fear.

In reality, people don't grow through studying and thinking — they mostly grow via what they do each and every day. By directly experiencing things, you can see how your newfound knowledge and understanding can be applied concretely to your life.

For example, most people worry about their first job and about interviewing for that job. They want everything to be perfect! But in order for something to be perfect, you need to experience the imperfect version of it. There is no other way around the issue. Yes, the ultimate goal is to have a successful job interview and then receive a job offer. But you only need one job — the right one. You don't need every interview to be successful, because there will be another interview. You can learn a lot from unsuccessful interviews...at least, if you really want to grow as a person.

Here's another example, this time in the sports world. In a soccer match, Team A may play well in general the whole time...but the result may be decided in the last few minutes, when Team B has settled down and become calm and is putting their best effort into the game. That's when Team B can turn the situation upside down and achieve victory. If Team B does that, everyone will acknowledge that Team B won the game, and Team B will receive much praise.

Results count! You only need one great interview. What you need to do is start actually going on job interviews instead of only preparing for them and worrying and becoming paralyzed. The great thing is that once you start doing interviews, you will realize you've done many unnecessary or impractical things during your preparations. Therefore, the more you interview, the less fear you'll feel and the more confident you'll become. In general, most people only receive one job offer for every ten interviews they do. (Sometimes it's only one offer for every 15 interviews.) Hence, everyone fails at least once if not a lot more often. That's completely normal.

The most important thing is to start doing. Do not procrastinate! And you don't need to label things as being a "success" or a "failure." Instead, be courageous and simply experience those feelings of success or failure and learn from each one of them. You just need to start!

Another thing you can start doing is let your mind relax each and every day, as guided by the script I've posted here.

https://viethungnguyen.com/2019/01/15/hay-thu-gian-lets-relax/

Once you can really let your mind relax, those brief moments of peace you'll attain will allow you to cultivate more positive energy and self-confidence. Those peaceful moments — although very brief — can help tell you what you need to do next.

Whose fault is it?

You may have heard a story like this: "A kid was playing in the house. He fell down on the floor, hurt and crying. His father found out that his son had fallen because of a toy car — the kid lost his mindfulness, stumbled over it, and fell. The father 'hit' the toy car, saying the car was at fault, in order to not blame the boy, thinking that it may help relieve the little one."

The story seems simple. However, it would be dangerous to just accept that "accusation." That's how cultures become blaming cultures: when people blame others and refuse to take personal responsibility.

We watch TV. We read the news. And most of the time, we overwhelmingly hear and see constant criticism about the weaknesses of government, of health care, of education, of everything. It is easy to point out the mistakes made by people around us. It is easy to criticize without offering any solutions. We criticize others in order to relieve our fears and to temper our anger at the chaos of life.

But does criticizing or blaming solve your problems or our greater society's problems? Unfortunately, most of the time, it doesn't. Yet those criticism and blaming can do one thing, and it's a big one: overwhelm you with insecurity and fear. Worse than that, those feelings are contagious — they start with you, but then spread to others.

I read a great advice somewhere that said, "If you are not part of the solution, you are part of the problem." Yes, that's very true.

Maybe you see many things that you think are wrong. If you do, then you need to ask yourself, "What can I do to change the situation?" If you can't find any solutions, step back and observe more. You may realize that you need to change your thoughts, change the way you see things, change your attitude toward those apparently negative things. That will certainly help you be more active and have more courage going forward instead of criticizing and blaming others and being overwhelmed by worries.

There is an old Chinese saying: "Once faced with difficulties, normal people blame those on others. Good people blame those on themselves. But great people blame no one." Truly wise people do not care whose fault it is. Instead, they try to investigate difficulties in order to understand what has happened. From there, they can see what they themselves can do to improve the situation.

So, stop! Stop criticizing and blaming. Instead, ask yourself, "What can I contribute?"

Don't lose faith in this world

In the current age of technology, we're all overwhelmed by media information from TV shows, newspapers, internet channels, social networks, etc. If you skim through those channels, you're likely bombarded with countless stories about scandals, problems with government, the erosion of ethics, extreme criminal cases, torrid stories about rich people, child trafficking, domestic abuse, the failures of education, the failures of healthcare, and on and on. All of those stories have one thing in common: they cultivate worries, insecurities, fears, and negative thoughts. Gradually, at some point, it becomes easy to lose faith in yourself and the world.

"But there are too many bad things out there! And they *do* have a direct impact on our lives!" you might be saying. Yes, I think those are valid concerns. I have no argument there. Yet I suggest this: do not allow those worries to steal your faith in this world. And I'm not talking about religious faith — I mean faith in the great nature of human beings, faith in kindness, faith that things always evolve. In other words, the aspects that make up a positive mindset.

Why do we have to be careful about losing our faith in this world? Because once you lose your faith, you start losing yourself. If you don't have a positive mindset, it means that negative thoughts are occupying your mind. It means that you will always see the world through the filter of negativity. As a result, then you always have doubts, negative thoughts, worries, and fears, and that in turn is why you are often unable to focus, work effectively, love, or contribute. Losing faith means losing your potential and the goodness inside of yourself.

So don't let negativity steal your faith! Stop feeding your mind with useless information. Knowing more negative information and news won't bring you peace and safety in this world. You can leverage the same Internet and the same technologies to search for stories about kindness and great people and organizations who are working on many meaningful projects for communities around the world. If you look for those stories, you'll find that they are also everywhere. They're just unfortunately not what media usually promotes.

So get out there! Meet and talk to those positive people. If you really want to find them, you will; if you pay attention to find them, you will gradually get to know them.

Go find those great movies and books that tell stories about great people with big hearts! Let your mind be filled with those meaningful stories.

Nurture and build faith in this world by working with positive people and getting to know their great stories. That way, you won't lose your own self.

1000

I happened to learn this from my co-worker: *"There are a thousand reasons for you not to do a thing. And there are the same number of reasons to convince you to do that same thing."* That conveys a simple, yet powerful message.

If you don't like something or you don't believe in something, you tend to see a thousand reasons telling you that it is bad and you don't need to do it. And the same is true for the opposite. But what if your belief is not right? If you put your belief in the wrong place, it will keep driving you toward making mistakes and harming yourself through your actions, thoughts, and statements.

In order to avoid this, I have a few suggestions:
- Try your best to maintain an open mind and to have a small ego. Sometimes that can be hard to do, but keep reminding yourself that there are many, many things in this world you don't know about. Keeping that in mind will help you have a more open attitude toward things happening around you.
- Try your best to maintain a positive attitude as you are giving serious thought to anything.
- Be mindful and ask yourself if what you're working on and what you believe in is harmful to people around you, including yourself. On many occasions, your desires and your anger may be harming yourself in subtle ways that

you don't realize.
- If you're angry or unsettled, don't make any decisions. Let your mind cool down first! You can only see things with clarity once your mind is calm and peaceful.

Maintaining an open mind, having a positive attitude, cultivating a state of calmness, and making sure your actions are not harmful to anyone (including yourself) are crucial for seeing things with clarity. Once you've done that, then use your thousand reasons to do the rest!

Victim mentality is a universal issue

I found these concepts in a book called *13 Things Mentally Strong Parents Don't Do*. Do you see yourself in any of these situations?

1. You think someone else — or some unfortunate circumstance — is preventing you from being your best.

2. You think other people are generally luckier and more fortunate than you are.

3. While certain solutions may work for other people, your problems are exceptional.

4. You spend a lot of time complaining about other people's behaviors and how they affect you.

5. You believe nothing ever goes right in your life.

Don't believe any of those things! If you do, you will have a victim mentality, and it will steal many opportunities as well as a lot of energy from you, making your life less beautiful than what it should be.

My responses to those five thoughts are these:

1. No one can block you from attaining happiness and success. Only you and your own thoughts are blocking you! Don't let that happen.

2. Yes, each of us has our own luck. Our lives are unique and different. However, you don't have to compare yourself to others as that may drag you down rather than help you. The beauty is that if you live a thoughtful and well-rounded life, you will have more opportunities to get to know more and more great people. *Then* you will have more and more luck. Being

thoughtful means that you harm no one, including yourself.

3. Each one of us has our own problems, and they all seem big to us. While you don't need to argue about your problems being bigger than other people's problems, you need to be open to listening to and learning from other people's problems and solutions. Then you can try to change yourself and your attitudes and thoughts in order to find suitable solutions for your own problems and challenges.

4. Complaining or blaming never brings us solutions, yet doing so can certainly make us exhausted, down, and more negative. So stop complaining and blaming.

5. You don't need to label things as being "right" or "wrong." That's not necessary. What is happening to you now is happening because of your previous thoughts, actions, and statements. If you want to have a better life, you have to improve your thoughts, actions, and your statements. Only then will life go your way.

Positive thinking vs. negative thinking

Why should we maintain positive thinking and try to remove negative thinking?

Self-confidence

While negative thinking will surely make you feel powerless and small in the midst of what's happening around you, positive thinking can give you a "can-do" attitude and the belief that (1) There is still hope; (2) There are still things we don't know about yet that can help us work through our challenges; and (3) There is always a better way to deal with our current challenges.

Calmness

While negative thinking will bring you insecurities, worries, and fears, positive thinking will bring you quietness and clarity, which are critically necessary to have when you're faced with life's challenges.

Energy

While negative thinking will steal much of your energy and leave you feeling burdened, positive thinking will give you more energy and the courage to move on.

Happiness

While negative thinking leads you to the dark side of your soul and leaves you with negative feelings that make you suffer, positive thinking helps you feel refreshed and recharged so that you can live your life to the fullest. Isn't that all part of the happiness journey that you have been and will be pursuing for a lifetime?

I'm not saying that everyone can drop all of their negative thoughts right here and now — that's not realistic. (I can't do that, either.) However, if you cultivate and nurture positive thoughts every day, doing so will certainly help you gradually remove negative thoughts and replace them with positive ones. As a result, you will be able to enjoy self-confidence, calmness, peace of mind, and happiness throughout your lifetime.

Who can bother me?

In the lobby of the KMS office on the way back from lunch, I met up with one of my old friends. We exchanged hellos and some joking questions. "What are you doing here?" I asked. And my friend said, "I'm here to bother you…"

That was just a joke, but it did spark a thought in my mind. In that moment, I replied, "Who can bother me?" That's an interesting thought.

Although everything is always happening to you and around you, from your perspective, you can only know what is happening by capturing data through your six senses. Let's call those your "sensors." Your sensors are your very first data gateways — they can insulate you from acquiring data as well as help you capture it. Once they sense something through your hearing, tasting, feeling, etc., all of that data is sent to your mind, where it will be presented to you after having been "filtered" through your knowledge and your prejudice.

You can see that the key to this process is how you interpret the captured data. Depending on how you do that, you might interpret the data as bothersome or entertaining, good or bad, likable or unappealing. If you can understand this process, I believe you can have a better and more positive influence over your own life, because then you can recondition your prejudices and thoughts to see things more clearly/differently.

It is true that no one can bother you except you, but usually we forget about that. A lot of people don't see the fact that they have the power *not* to let anything bother them. This can be achieved by seeing more and more of the real truth and changing your thoughts, attitudes, and responses to what is happening to you in ways that are more beneficial to you and your life. People can hate you and get angry at you, yes, *but* you can see through that and understand why they feel that way. Not only will you gain empathy for them, then their hostility can't bother you.

Remember, only *you* can bother *you*. And if you're aware of this and adjust your thoughts, attitudes, and responses regarding what is happening around you and to you, then one day, no one (including yourself!) can bother you any longer.

With reading comes miracles

A few years ago, I published a slide deck titled ***"Why do you have to read?"*** to urge people to read and to read more. Today, I got this amazingly beautiful surprise of a moving story from my co-worker.

"Hi anh Hung,
There are two stories I want to share with you.
The first story is this: The husband of my high school friend was in a traffic incident two years ago and suffered serious brain damage. At that time, my friend was raising her three-year-old daughter and working in Hanoi. Every week, she traveled to her husband's hometown to visit her husband, who was being taken care by his family.
The second story is this: My sister got married recently. After just a few months, her husband was killed in an incident and she became a widow when she was very young.
I'm very close to both my friend and my sister, and they had both run into giant hurdles in their lives. They became stuck and lost their direction. Everyone tried to encourage them, but it didn't seem to be working, probably because no one could fully understand their situations and what they had experienced.
I can't offer expert solutions, but I did recommend doing one thing: take time to calm the mind and read. I bought an Alezaa[1] premium account for my friend and attached a note that she should pick out a book and spend time reading it.

---

[1] A Vietnamese eBook store

And something wonderful has happened — she feels much better! She has regained her motivation to work and enjoy her life with her loved ones. My sister still needs more time to calm down and more time to read, but I believe that she will ultimately experience the same wonderful sense of peace.

Again, thank you a lot for influencing me and others to read! That's how we can seek our own solutions in this world.

Have a nice weekend."

I had never thought I would receive a wonderful note like this for having inspired people to read. When I did get it, though, I was overwhelmed and even more convinced that reading can help people heal.

And so I've kept trying to convince people to read. Books can't help with all situations, but sometimes they can bring about miracles!

"The truth will set you free…"

I heard this meaningful lyric when I turned on my music one morning: "The truth will set you free…"

Freedom comes from wisdom. Wisdom comes from knowing the truth — real truth, not the truth or the justice you see in the news. Those are too noisy.

What would make you happy? What is the meaning of your life? Do you know those deep truths about yourself? The more you learn about those truths, the more freedom you can attain, and freedom is your pathway to happiness. Truthful happiness!

I certainly call this happiness

This is the email I wrote to my co-workers on the seventh anniversary of the company I co-founded, KMS Technology Vietnam.

"Dear all KMSers,

I got Quynh's status in the morning reminding me that today is the official anniversary day for KMS. It's been seven years — today we're turning eight!

When I looked at all of the photos we captured at our year-end party 2015 just last Friday, I was immediately overwhelmed by all of the laughter and joyful moments. We had a great night! And that is certainly the result of the great work of a great team called KMSers over the last seven years.

I tried to gather all of the photos I'm in among the 750+ photos captured during the party. All I see is happiness in my own eyes, lots of happiness.

I believe that if you likewise gather your own pictures,

you'll see the same: happiness.

Looking ahead, I see the same thing: HAPPINESS! For all of us.

Our happiness is not something we inherit from God — our happiness comes from our teamwork and the bright minds we have here in this group called the KMSers. I'm blessed that I have a chance to work with such a great team, KMSers! I'm so very thankful for that."

Happy Thanksgiving 2014

Thanksgiving is not celebrated in Vietnam, yet as I have worked with partners and clients in the US over the years, I have also come to look forward to Thanksgiving.

While I don't roast a turkey, I always do one thing to celebrate the day. As the name "Thanksgiving" suggests, I'd like to take the chance now to give thanks. Words can't express exactly how I feel, but at least they can convey my general message.

First of all, I'd like to send my thankfulness to my parents and my in-laws, who brought us into this life and who raised us to be the "us" we are today.

Secondly, I'd like to thank my dear wife, who has been with me for the last 20 years. That's a long enough time, right? You are not just my partner, you are also my mentor. I think I am very fortunate to have you in my life.

Then, I'd like to thank my little daughter. My dear little princess, you have brought us countless happiness moments and many, many lessons about how we can become better parents and better human beings. I have learned and grown a lot from being with you and will always learn and grow with you! Ah... You are another "teacher" in my life.

Next, I'd like to thank all of the KMS Technology staff, those who are current employees as well as those who have left. Over the past six years, it has been my privilege to have the chance to know you, to work with you, and to enjoy many precious moments with you. I have enjoyed spending time with you so much that the KMS staff has become my second family. It's a big one!

And finally, I would like to thank all of my friends and relatives. People usually see me as a happy person. And do you want to know why? Because I have you as friends and relatives! You have given me much happiness in this life.

If you also think giving thanks is something we should do on Thanksgiving, do it! Together, we can show more and more of our appreciation to our loved ones on this occasion.

Thanks and Happy Thanksgiving!

Dealing with sadness

Whenever you feel uncomfortable, sad, or disappointed, pause yourself. Try to observe the feeling, the sensation you are feeling in your body and mind. Why are you sad? How burdened do you feel? Are you feeling regret? Disappointment? Do you feel impotent or insecure? Can you change what has happened? Or are you stuck in an infinite loop of "I wish that…" or "If I only… " inside your mind?

Let your body and mind really reach the bottom of the sadness. If you need to cry, cry. Once you can be directly in touch with your suffering and your sadness and can talk with them, your body and mind will start to tell you the way out.

Whether you want it or not, sadness will eventually end. Don't try to hold it back! In an objective reality, that sadness doesn't belong to you — it's just a natural part of the thinking process. In reality, nothing can stay with us forever.

Sadness and joy are natural processes of the mind. They happen in a natural and independent manner depending on what has happened previously. We can only resolve our sadness, our disappointment, and our dissatisfaction if we can stop identifying those as being "ours." Once you have walked away from them, look back — that's when you can more clearly see what *has* happened and *is* happening, how you can / should view it, and how you can accept it. After you've really made those observations about yourself and you have a truer understanding of why your sadness happened, you can open your mind and adopt a positive attitude. With your new understanding, you can drop your sadness, unburdening your mind; from there, you can more easily (and positively) see what you need to do and how you can prevent that sadness from happening again.

Don't run away from your sadness, and don't ignore it. You can't escape having sadness in your life! Do face your sadness directly and observe it deeply. That's the best way to "solve" it.

What lies behind difficulties

Challenges, difficulties, and misfortunes are an inevitable part of life. I think everyone would agree with that statement. However, each of us deals with difficulties differently. Illness, bankruptcy, broken relationships, loss of assets, death of a loved one… anything can happen at any time without any warning. Depending on how we respond to those unwanted events, they can either help us grow or not. The challenge is that many times we don't see the hidden meanings behind what has happened to us. I happened to bump into this meaningful story on the Internet:

A man was the sole survivor of a shipwreck. He was stranded on a small desert island with only the items from his ship that had washed up on the shore with him. The man carefully constructed a small hut to store his few precious belongings and to protect himself from the weather.

One day as he was standing in the ocean fishing for his next meal, he turned back to shore to see that his hut was on fire and smoke was billowing into the air. The worst was happening! "God, how could you do this to me?" he cried. He believed that all was lost.

Later, he heard the sound of an approaching ship in the distance coming to rescue him.

"How did you know I was here?" the man asked his rescuers.

"We saw your smoke signal," they replied.

What lies behind your difficulties? Certainly, it's

hard to find the answer to that question once everything has become a mess. But if you can be mindful about the fact that you need to keep calm and deal with whatever difficulty you come across, then you can capture all the wonders of this life.

And don't forget that we need to learn from the small and the big lessons that continuously come into our lives! We need to learn lessons from our successes as well as lessons from our failures.

In short, behind difficulties, you have the opportunity to learn, to grow, and to move forward to new opportunities that await you. In other words, keep on learning, growing, and maturing.

Giving or receiving?

The remote villages of Long An province, close to the border with Cambodia, was the destination for one of our KMS charity trips. Besides the gifts we were bringing for the disadvantaged families, we were prepared to offer 14 grants to students who had good academic performances. We had offered grants before, but this time, we wanted to deliver those grants right to the students' houses.

The houses were very temporary. Some of them didn't have regular walls — instead, big pieces of canvas covered bamboo poles to make the sides of the house. Some of the houses didn't have enough canvas to create four entire walls, and the winds and rain could easily flow through the whole house.

Most of the students who were getting the grants this time were from very poor and disadvantaged families. Their stories often went something like what we heard that day:

The family had three daughters. When the mother was pregnant with the third one, knowing that it was a girl, the father forced the mother to "remove" her daughter. The "removing" effort failed and left the third daughter with permanent lifetime stigma. The father then left the family and married a new wife in order to have a son.

The three siblings grew up with their grandma. The first sibling had already dropped out of school and was working. She could earn about 25 cents a day to add to the family's food fund.

The grandma was sharing this particular story with us and had to pause as she cried in the middle of it.

The middle sibling was the one who got the grant. Once she had accepted the envelope containing the grant, the girl gave us a short thank-you speech: "I'd like to thank you for giving this to me. I promise to try my best, to be deserving of this gift..." Her voice faltered as she too broke out in tears. Soon enough, every one of us in the room also had tears in our eyes.

Were we giving or receiving on this trip? Though these grants are very small gifts, they have a positive influence and serve as encouragement. But is giving the grants all we achieve?

When we as a company take these trips, instead of doing what we usually do on a Saturday — sipping coffee at home, reading, or sleeping — we spend meaningful time together, observe and learn from the direct experiences our trips give us. Our hearts beat hard when we hear the villagers' stories. We hurt, too. Our tears are heartfelt. Those real stories give us countless unforgettable moments. Though the students who receive our grants are in extremely difficult situations, they are still trying their best to study.

I think what we give the villagers is less than the lessons we learn from them, deep and moving lessons. We are the ones who receive the most. And that is the biggest reward for doing any charity project.

Live and die

There is an absolute truth that no one can argue: death is inevitable for everyone. In addition to that, no one knows for sure when it will happen — life is full of unexpected and sudden events.

We can't ignore those truths, and since we can't ignore them, we should accept them in the most positive manner possible. I used to hear people say, "If at the end we'll die anyway, then we should spend whatever we have (money, health, etc.) before it's too late."

I suggest you think about the situation a little bit differently. If you can wake up in the morning and enjoy having breakfast and sipping a cup of coffee, you should be quietly thankful and start the day with a full heart. You should maximize the time that you have now, in the present, to meaningfully live. Support, love, and care for your family, your loved ones, your friends, your co-workers, and your communities.

Live in a way that even if you have to leave this world suddenly, you won't have regrets, because you will have left many meaningful things behind. You can't bring anything with you once you die — you can only leave them for others. Be sure to leave those meaningful things for who stays, for the next generations, and for your children.

Because that day of departure could come suddenly, you'd better exploit each and every minute in the now to do your best to contribute to this world!

The little me

I've learned an important thing during the course of my personal development journey: once you start getting older, your ego needs to become smaller. If you see yourself going in the opposite direction, I suggest you stop and reflect upon yourself and where you're heading.

Some people become more and more stubborn as they get older. They believe they already understand how things work. They believe that they're right when they judge the people around them. Unfortunately, that stubbornness only can help them do one thing: build up a giant me. That me is the root of problems, insecurities, and burdens.

I learned this quote from the monk ***Thich Thanh Nghiem***: *"Remember this: as you are born and while you grow up and when you go away from this life, you are very small in this world."* Yes, that is true. It's good to understand that concept in order to remember that our knowledge about life is very little — we're tiny beings in the eyes of Mother Nature. This reminds us to keep an open mind and learn about what and who surrounds us.

When your me becomes smaller, that means you are exploring happiness in this big, wild world, one step at a time. That's certainly a lifetime journey for anyone!

Learn and observe from nature

The power of nature and its instincts within every living thing is always a wonder. However, because of our limited knowledge and our unlimited greediness and anger, humans usually go against the laws of nature. What a pity!

As a result of that, illnesses in our bodies and especially our minds become worse and worse every day. We need to stop, let our minds rest, and then truly seek what Mother Nature has granted us right inside our own bodies and minds.

Alone

"Being alone is necessary for me to get in touch with my innermost being. If we are not in touch with ourselves, how can we be in touch with others? Not being in touch with ourselves is the cause of not being in touch with others, which is why most people are lonely." – Excerpted from **Snow in the Summer** of **Sayadaw U Jotika**

Being alone may be the biggest fear that most of us have. Usually, we will try to escape that by seeking out all sorts of entertainment or by using addictive substances. But these are just temporary covers. Ultimately, we still have to face being alone, when we are old and sickness is on our way.

Being in touch with your body and mind is the most effective, most direct, and most complete way to deal with loneliness.

Mosquito bite

Everybody gets bitten by a mosquito at least once. When it happens, a small red dot appears on your skin. It itches and makes you want to scratch it. Your skin becomes abraded and sore.

But have you ever tried this? Say the mosquito is flying around you. You don't swat at it, and the mosquito finally manages to land on your hand and start biting you. You try to observe the process without interrupting him. After it's had enough "food," the mosquito flies away. You continue observing how your body responds to the bite. Can you imagine what happens next?

I accidentally experienced that situation once, when I did not try swat the mosquito. After a while, I started to have a strange feeling in my elbow. I looked down and saw that a mosquito friend had landed silently on my elbow and started to investigate the area to find where he should sink in his stinger. And then he pushed it down into my skin.

Nothing hurt. Moments passed by. The mosquito's stomach became bigger and redder. Trying to keep my elbow still, I tried to get out my phone to take a picture. Maybe I moved a little too quickly, because the mosquito flew away immediately.

At that moment, I didn't see any mark on my elbow — the itching and the small red dot appeared a little later. I tried not to scratch the bite and not to think about it, to go back to work instead. The bite continued itching. But surprisingly, after a while, the itching disappeared. And the bite itself disappeared before I even knew it, before I could even capture a picture of it. No trace left.

If I had responded in the usual way and had scratched over and over again, then a rash definitely would have appeared, and it probably would have become bigger and stayed there for a few days. It could have even left a little scar on my elbow.

At work and in our life, the same thing often happens — we have unnecessary conflicts, disagreements, and arguments with co-workers and our loved ones, and many times, those little and unnecessary conflicts turn into bigger conflicts and leave some big scars on our relationships. But if you know when to stop and do nothing, then those conflicts disappear before you know it. Even better, they don't leave behind any scars!

Sometimes, by not doing anything, you can avoid many unnecessary troubles.

Stillness

Imagine you are right next to a big, beautiful lake early in the morning. You're surrounded by trees. The air is cool and pure. The lake's surface is utterly still, just like a mirror — a big, natural one. The clouds and the sky are clearly reflected in its surface. What a beautiful scene! If you drop a small rock into the lake, you can see concentric ripples of water spreading away from you. How gorgeous!

But if it were a rainy, windy day, the surface of the lake would be surging and tumultuous. Then would you be able to see the clouds and sky reflected? Would you be able to see those beautiful concentric circles when you dropped a small rock into the lake?

Of course, you wouldn't be able to see any of that — the lake's surface would be upset and angry, beaten by the wind and rain.

That lake's surface is similar to our minds. If your mind is always surging with crashing waves caused by negative thoughts and feelings, are you sensitive enough to feel and observe what is happening in your life? Of course you aren't, because your mind is fully occupied by upset and anger.

In contrast, if you can keep your mind still and quiet, it's easy for you to feel and observe anything that happens to you and around you in a clear, serene manner. That's when you can realize the deeper meanings hidden behind the challenges and difficulties that life continuously throws your way.

Meditation can help you bring back and maintain stillness in your mind. Actively letting your mind rest or relax can help bring stillness and quietness into your mind, too, or you can seek out and enjoy calming things in nature, like early sunrises (or sunsets) on the beach or views of mountains. Even simpler, just listen to the sounds of nature around you, like the sound of the wind going through the trees. Or smell the scent of flowers in the air.

If you can be in touch with nature as it happily exists around you, stillness and quietness will softly move into your mind.

The nose

You may have come across a scenario where a young man is told, "People say you're brutal." He immediately stands up, angrily looks around, and then shouts, "Who? Who? Who said that? I'm not brutal! Who said that? I'll kick their ass."

One way we might describe this man's reaction would be "he's not able to see his own nose" or "he's not able to see his own back." Too many times, we don't see our mistakes, whether we're purposely ignoring them or not. We may not see them because we lack information, knowledge or wisdom. Or sometimes we simply can't see our mistakes because we are stubborn, arrogant, or overconfident. And many of us run into these situations quite often. We need a mirror.

The mirror we need is our knowledge, our wisdom, and our maturity. If we can keep our mind calm so that we can find our "mirror" and gaze into it when difficulties pop up, we are more able to see through those difficulties with clarity.

Are you able to see your nose?

The fish and the turtle

The following is a great story I learned from a book about Buddhism.

Once upon a time, there was a fish. She didn't know anything else except what was in the water because the water was her whole world. One day, as she was swimming around the lake like she did on any other day, she met up with her long-time friend, the turtle. "Hey, hello! It's been a long time. Where did you go?" she asked.

"Hey, my lovely little friend! I've been on dry land for the last few days," replied the turtle.

"Dry land? What is that? How come the land is dry? I haven't seen anything that's dry. Dry land must have nothing on it."

Gently, the turtle replied, "If you want to think about it that way, it's okay. But the place where I went is truly dry land."

"Can you tell me more?" the fish asked curiously. "How come the land is dry? What is it like? Is it humid?"

"No, dry land is not humid."

"Is dry land cool and soft and comfortable?"

"No, it's not cool, and it's not soft or comfortable, either."

"Is dry land transparent? Can light go through it?"

"No, dry land is not transparent. Light cannot go through it."

"Is it comfortable for us to swim in dry land?"

"No, we can't swim in dry land."

"Is it moving and flowing in a stream?"

"No, it's not moving or flowing in a stream."

"Can dry land create waves and shatter into bubbles?"

"No..."

The fish was starting to lose her calm. She suddenly showed her joyful arrogance and shouted out loud, "See! What I thought is true! I said dry land is nothing. I asked and you confirmed that dry land is not humid, not cool, not comfortable, and not transparent. Dry land can't move and can't flow; it can't create waves or bubbles. So therefore, it is nothing, isn't it?"

The turtle replied, "My lovely little friend, if you insist that dry land is nothing, then continue thinking so. But anyone familiar with water and with dry land would know that you are a novice fish, because you insist that anything that you don't know about can't exist. But that's only because you haven't ever known it."

Then the turtle left the fish and started swimming away, thinking about making another trip to the dry land that the fish thought didn't exist.

This kind of situation happens over and over again in our lives. One good example is meditation. It's hard to explain the benefit of meditation to those who haven't meditated yet. However, when you see the peacefulness of people who *do* meditate, you can trust that what they're doing is beneficial and you can become more open to exploring how meditation can help you. You, too, can gain more knowledge and peacefulness!

A cloud has no legs

The image of cloud without any legs is meant to show that there is no anchor for any cloud in the big blue sky. This is a great image to express the fact that in life, everything comes and goes. Watch a darkening stormy sky right before the rain. In that moment, you mostly see darkness and looming pressure, right? What else do you see?

If you focus on the sky, you certainly only will see darkness and sadness. And your mind will be overwhelmed with those sensations. However, if you focus on seeing the whole picture — which is the movement of the clouds through the sky — you will start to realize a few different things.

You will start to see continuous big rolls of clouds coming and going through the sky. Right behind them is still the big blue sky. Beautiful movement, isn't it? You could record video of it in time-lapse mode and see exactly what I mean: behind those dark and brutal clouds, there always lies a vast, peaceful, and bright blue sky.

The truth is that everything is moving and changing. Nothing ever stands still, whether you want to believe it will or not. Whether you see it or not, things are continuously changing and moving. The beauty is that if we mindfully stay within those movements and those changes, we can see things more purely and with more clarity.

If you don't see those changes, you miss seeing

the bigger picture of everything. You miss seeing that behind clouds and darkness, there is always a big blue sky holding peace and tranquility. That peace and tranquility are always there.

Can you see it? Clouds have no legs. There is nothing for a cloud to attach to. Therefore, if it comes, it must go. It must eventually leave, yet the peaceful, calm, beautiful sky always stays.

It's the same with life. Many times, we bump into sadness, depression, difficulties, and challenges that seem insurmountable. We are temporarily overwhelmed by them, similar to those dark clouds that seem to be fully filling up the sky. We feel stuck and depressed.

But you should always remind yourself that sadness and difficulties don't have any legs — whether you want them to or not, they will come to an end, one way or another. Don't get "lost" in those clouds. You only need to watch them and thoroughly feel them. After a while, you will start seeing things more clearly as you uncover the big blue sky behind them.

Also note that joyfulness is like sadness — it comes and goes, too. That's how nature works. The most effective thing we can do is simply observe these visitors as they come and go by in a calm and peaceful manner. Then you can completely "sip" from each moment of your life in a meaningful and useful way.

Peace comes from living by a code of ethics

I came across this wise concept somewhere: *"If you fail to adhere to ethics, you lose the peacefulness of your mind. And that makes meditation increasingly difficult, even in the most conducive environment. You need to have a solid basis of ethics before you can be strong and determined and face all of the suffering in your body and mind."*

This is a quite simple and understandable concept, yet we often forget it due to our greed, selfishness, or fear. And then we harm ourselves because of our greed, selfishness, or fear. It becomes an infinite loop of suffering.

Each of us has our own life to live. And we should fully live *our* life, not anyone else's. People can have their own judgments about our life, but those judgments should not be that too important to us. They could be references for us, yes, but they should not drive our own individual lives.

The truth is that no one can completely understand someone else's life or situation. That means that no one can fairly judge someone else's life. Each of us needs to be responsible for our own life and our own situation. By understanding ourselves (our thoughts, actions, and statements) more and more each day, we can make necessary changes so that we can live a better life.

How do we do that? It is a simple answer, yet it's not easy to do. The answer lies in how well we observe what is happening inside our mind and our body. That is the key.

As human beings, we make mistakes every day. At the same time, those mistakes offer us many chances to learn, adjust, grow, and become a better person. A mistake in and of itself is not that bad. That said, *not* learning from mistakes or making repeated mistakes is really bad.

Once we do something bad or unethical or we make a mistake, we don't feel right inside our mind and body. By continuously and thoroughly observing ourselves inwardly and in a sensible way, we can detect those not-right moments and we can stop whatever we are doing / thinking / saying, therefore no longer harming ourselves or others. Again, the key is observation.

And here is where maintaining a code of ethics comes into the picture. Thinking, doing, and speaking ethically are a means to purify your mind and bring it back to a tranquil and peaceful mental state. Once that happens, your senses are sharper, and as a result of *that*, it's easier for you to catch those not-right feelings and sensations and know when to learn, adjust, and grow so that you can become a better person. Then you will be on your journey to attaining peace and happiness.

The beauty is that this whole process starts with you, not anywhere else. Living an ethical life sends a powerful and meaningful message to everyone around us!

Is there one person to trust and love me?

I used to hear this question from one of my friends when she complained about her life. "I only need to have one person to trust and love me," she would say longingly. "Is there one person to trust and love me?"

My immediate response was, "You don't need anyone to trust and love you — you only need *you* to trust and love you. That's more than enough! Besides, if you don't trust and love yourself, who else can?"

The answer to this question is implied in the question itself. If you can build up your self-confidence and if you really know how to love yourself and care for yourself, then people around you will respect you. And from there, they can start to trust you and love you.

Another truth is that if you know how to love yourself, you will never harm anyone else, because while selfishness, greed, anger, and hatred are what bring negative and harmful things into our lives, selfishness, greed, anger and hatred are never included in the concept of love.

In order for someone to trust you and love you, first and foremost, you need to trust yourself, respect yourself, and love yourself. That's the essential pre-requisite for a better and happier life. If you start from this simple place, you'll have a better life.

"What did I do wrong for more than half of my life?"

One time, my friend asked me if I could help her figure out what she had done wrong in her life. She was about 40, and she felt she had lived half of her life already. She was depressed and felt that she was finding more and more dead ends in her life.

It was obvious that if she kept on doing what she had been doing (i.e., having the same thoughts, doing the same actions, and making the same statements), then her future would be the same or even much worse than it had been. She needed to change. And she needed to start by changing her thoughts, her actions, and her statements.

If you find yourself in a similar situation and you feel stuck even though you think you haven't done anything wrong, you need to think through the situation again. And you need to change. Change is certainly not an easy thing! However, it's the only way to liberate yourself from suffering. Buddhism is one approach you could take — it offers a way to alleviate your suffering — or you could find your own way of making changes.

The great part is that you only need to start with yourself right here and now. You don't need to go anywhere else to start; you don't need to seek a solution anywhere else. You just need to start inside yourself, right here and now.

Alleviate suffering

Everything comes and goes; everything is born and dies. That's the source of suffering.

Once we have something joyful, we become attached to it and we're afraid that it will go away someday. But here's the truth: no matter how much we worry, it will go away.

Or if we're dissatisfied with something, we become angry and wish that things had not happened that way. The better thing to do in this situation is: (1) Try to understand why it happened that way; (2) Learn from that and commit to not cultivating the kind of thoughts, actions, or statements that would make it happen again (or at least try to limit it from happening again); and (3) Be mindful and patient and continuously observe what happens next. The dissatisfaction will come to an end just as everything else does.

With calmness and mindful observation, we can choose how we respond to dissatisfaction in order to not cultivate more "bad seeds" for our future. That way, we will better benefit our body and mind.

A dog and a piece of bone

I once bumped into a little cute puppy who was very focused on what he was doing. In that moment, I was reminded of a lesson from *Monk Ajahn Chah*. There was only a bone — nothing else was left — but the dog was still working very hard on it and spending a lot of time on it.

We find ourselves in that situation many times: we are very focused on what we're doing, yet we're wasting a lot of time. Often, we're doing things that don't help us to grow or become a better person, yet we think that we are "eating" a lot. It's better to leave that bone alone!

Unconditional love

Flowers do a very good job of brightening our lives and bringing joyfulness to us without asking for anything in return. This is unconditional love. Learning this kind of love from flowers can allow us to have a more fulfilled and beautiful life. Just like flowers.

Joyfulness comes from what we do, not necessarily from the outcome of it

Good morning, new day! Good morning to the new flourishing flower. It is so beautiful! I've realized that I have directly experienced a meaningful concept through gardening. Gardening is about being patient and having the discipline to water and care for plants. Of course, whether they flourish or not is the job of the plants, not the gardener — sometimes plants are independent of the gardener's wishes. Hence, once they are flourishing, try to enjoy them in that very moment!

Even if plants don't flourish, gardeners still can enjoy watering and watching over them every day. It's similar to having meals each and every day — even if you don't like to eat, you still have to eat something for your body, and you might as well be eating joyfully.

In short, joyfulness comes from daily caring. That's how it thrives!

Yen Tu challenge

Yen Tu mountain is over 1,000 meters tall, with thousands of stone steps to the top. It takes nearly four hours to ascend the staircases. When I climbed them, I got several great lessons and insights. And I'm going to share those with you!

During a trip to Hanoi to receive the Sao Khue award for KMS Technology Vietnam, I decided to do something different. I had heard about Yen Tu mountain, where many great pagodas and temples were built starting in the reign of King Tran Nhan Tong in the 13th century. I thought it would be a great experience to explore the mountain and the Dong Pagoda at the very top of it.

I flew from Saigon to Hanoi on a Friday night. The flight was delayed, and I got to Hanoi late. (I went to bed at 1:30 a.m.) I woke up at 5:30 a.m., had breakfast, and was ready to go at 6:20. At 9:30, I arrived at the foot of Yen Tu mountain.

I was 37 years old at that time and in good health. I carried two bottles of water and a Canon DSLR camera with me. This was the first time I was going to make the trek up, and based on what I had learned via the internet, it was going to take four to six hours to summit the mountain.

Fast or slow?

I eagerly got started, climbing fast and feeling excited by the challenge. However, after only 30 minutes or so, I felt like I couldn't move my legs anymore. And I knew that I still had several more hours to reach the top! I started to count: 1, 2, 3… stop…switch legs and start again…1, 2, 3…stop… switch…again and again. Then I waited a bit before starting the process again.

Fast or slow? Which one is better? Neither of them, I realized. The best speed is the most suitable speed. And my starting pace was not suitable — after all, I had become exhausted after only 30 minutes.

This lesson is very true in life. Fast or slow — which one is better? Neither. The best choice is the most suitable choice. Many times, you have to be fast; other times, you have to be slow. Very often, you need to be somewhere in between: neither fast nor slow. It depends on what you want to do, the context, the situation, and your condition.

On that day, in order to continue climbing to the top of Yen Tu, I had to adjust my pace correspondingly if I wanted to finish the trek.

You think you are strong? Think twice.

After changing my tactics, I continued my walk, but a bit more slowly. On the way, a group of seniors caught up to me. They quickly walked past me toward the top.

I observed that one of the ladies in the group seemed to be older than the rest. I tried to overhear their conversations out of curiosity. "How old are you?" a man asked the lady on the way down. "Seventy-four," she replied.

Well! That gave me a great boost. I can't imagine

how I will look at 74. Will I be as healthy as that lady obviously is?

That's something to think about. While I can't change the fact that my body is getting older, I'm certain that if I take care of my health today, I will be in better shape once I am older. Yes, I can make that happen today! You can only change the future starting with what you do today, right in this moment. Think about it. If you don't act in this present moment, how could you hope to have good health or a great future tomorrow?

Once I had nearly gotten to the top of Yen Tu (I was about a hundred meters away), I bumped into another group of people. They were sitting and resting on a big stone. One of them was an older charming lady with a great smile. I started talking to her and found out that she had started climbing up from the foot of Yen Tu at 9 a.m. It was now around 12:30 p.m., so it had taken about 3.5 hours for her to get this high. And this was the second time she was climbing the mountain! She was from Hanoi.

"How old are you?" I asked her. "Nearly 80 — I'm 79 now," replied the lady.

I laughed happily at hearing that and asked her if I could take a photo of her to show to young people in order to inspire them to undertake the same trek one day.

If you think you're strong, think twice and challenge yourself to be like her! It's not hard to do, but you will need to be disciplined. Exercise regularly, at least three times per week for 30 minutes each time, and make sure you sweat. Pick any sport — soccer, badminton, tennis, swimming — or do something easy, like running or even walking. Isn't that simple? Just do it now.

Team vs. individual?

I continued trekking slowly up the mountain. A group of young people caught up to me next, and I decided to silently join them, tagging along at the rear. I felt great! I no longer felt like I was alone — I belonged to a group and was encouraged by the power of the crowd. As a result of that, I had to push myself to walk harder and faster to keep pace with the group so that I was not left behind.

After a while, I started questioning myself. Did I really have to push myself like that? It was good exercise, yet was it the right thing to do? Was it the only way to maximize my capabilities?

I didn't have the answer, but I did know that I didn't want to be left behind. I walked faster and kept up with the pace of the group because I didn't want to lose face with these people who didn't even know that I was following them. But that was also the reason I didn't feel right about the situation and why I started questioning myself.

I was walking not because of me, but because of others. That made me really think. In life, many times, we don't really live our lives — we live someone else's life. We just follow the inertia of what others do or ask us to do. Often, the ultimate driver for us to strive every day is to be as good as others, as rich as others, as famous as others (if not more so). We do what we do because of others, not because of or for ourselves.

We should all think more about this. Do we want to live other peoples' lives, or do we want to live our own lives? If you want to live yours, stop and think more about it. Don't let the inertia or demands of others confuse and control your life. You're unique and special in this world, and you need to seek to understand more about yourself so that you can live your own life, one that's meaningful for *you*.

After having that realization, I decided to separate from the group at the next T-junction. At first, I didn't know if that was a good decision or not. I was surrounded by fog and couldn't see anything beyond ten meters, and on that day, not many people were trekking up the mountain. Basically, if I left the group, I was going to be on my own. Being alone is always scary, isn't it? Especially on a rainy day in the middle of the forest and on the side of a mountain.

The more I've thought about this since then, the more I've learned. Yes, we're often surrounded by friends and family and other people, but really, we spend most of our time alone with...ourselves. Think about that. Often, you're not alone because you don't have people around you — you're alone because no one around you understands you. That's not abnormal.

Most of us are alone in our minds. At any point in time, the only person you really have to deal with and spend time with is you. Period. The great thing about that is that being alone can help you ponder life more deeply to find your truths.

I am my own biggest challenge. The biggest challenges I could ever face are inside of me. I get angry. I get bored. I get tired. What can I do about it? That's a big question and I don't address it here, but nevertheless, I have to learn to deal with those challenges each and every day.

Going back to the trek, after a few moments of hesitating and worrying, I decided to just go ahead and separate from the group at the next junction.

Frankly, during many moments of the trek, I thought of quitting — no one would know, except for my inner me. He would know if I quit. My legs and body were so tired! Then I asked myself why had I decided to do this in the beginning? Why had I decided to go all the way to the top? With that as a reminder, I firmly decided to challenge myself to finish what I had started. Keep going, baby, keep going!

Focus on the next few steps while assuring you're going in the right direction.

Many times during the climb, I heard people ask the ones going down "How long far to get to the top?" or "How much longer to get to Dong Pagoda?" I was tracking the trek with my cell phone using Google's My Track. While I didn't ask those questions, a few times I did open my phone trying to see where I was on the map and how much farther I needed to walk. Same question, different mechanism.

Once I thought more about that, I realized

something else. Does it really help to look around and ask such a question? People might answer "Nearly there" but might be speaking an untruth in an attempt to motivate the people who are still climbing. Others may tell the truth and say that the top is still far away. But why do we ask? Whatever the answer may be, I still have to climb. That doesn't change. However, if I lose focus and keep looking for unhelpful information, it does take away a bit of my energy each time I do it.

The lesson I realized from this is that if you decide to do one thing, just focus on the next few steps while assuring that you are navigating toward the right direction. That's it! That way, it's much easier and more effective for you to do things. Don't waste your energy by looking around in search of unnecessary answers. This works very well in all occasions, including when you're conducting business.

You can't express it — people have to experience it!

And here's the final thing. I felt overwhelmed by being on the top of the mountain and by the entire trek. Although I couldn't see farther than ten meters, it was just beautiful to be up there. I took quite a few pictures using both my Canon and my phone. Later, though, I found out that those pictures were not as beautiful as what I had seen. How could a camera capture everything? It may be able to capture information like colors and shapes, but it fails to capture a lot of other things. Even if I were a great photographer, it was not realistic to expect a camera to be able to capture everything.

Being on the mountain was stunning. No words can express that feeling. Nobody else can feel that feeling unless they climb the mountain and directly experience it for themselves.

If you want to share something great with anyone, do not just tell them the story and do not just share the pictures — instead, encourage them to actually do it themselves. The best experiences happen by doing, not by hearing about something or reading about it or seeing someone's photos of it.

Yen Tu mountain is over 1,000 meters tall, with thousands of stone steps go up the top. During my four hours of climbing, I experienced several great lessons and insights. I suggest you, yes you, climb the mountain as well! I'm certain that you'll like it, too.

Life is a school without a graduation ceremony

Many lessons come our way each and every day. Like a teaching from *Sayadaw U Jotika* says, life is a school with lesson after lesson after lesson. There is no graduation ceremony. Once you finish learning a lesson, you have to learn the next one. If you haven't finish learning a lesson, life will bring that lesson back to you in a different form until you have learned it.

These lessons are continuous and nonstop. That's why there is no need to call something a "success" or a "failure," no need to label something as "good" or "bad" or refer to "happiness" or "suffering." Each is purely a lesson followed by another lesson. Learn those lessons well! That's how we grow up in this world. That's our spiritual journey.

"Relationship is the source of the greatest joy and the greatest mental suffering.

The quality of our life depends much on the quality of our relationship with people around us." — Excerpted from the book named **Snow in the Summer** by *Sayadaw U Jotika*

Yes, that is right! The biggest lesson we need to learn and experience each day in order to get closer to our own happiness is that the quality of the relationships we have with the people around us is really the quality of our own lives.

Unfortunately, most of the time, those relationships don't yield what we expect them to; we might even be disappointed by how people treat us.

Only once we can thoroughly understand the law of cause and effect (karma, dharma, or whatever term we use) can we accept what we are experiencing. Then we can pick the best option and respond to unexpected circumstances thrown at us in a noble and positive manner. That is how we grow.

It's very hard to change others, and although it's easier to change ourselves, that isn't easy, either. But changing ourselves is easier since we have more influence over ourselves than others do. (Hopefully!)

To change ourselves for the better, we need to carefully observe our body and mind and make appropriate changes that allow us to escape from the labels of "good" versus "bad," "happiness" versus "suffering," "success" versus "failure." As ***Monk Ajahn Brahm*** has taught us, we should not bend the truth according to our subjectivism. Instead, we should bend *ourselves* according to the objective truth that we can clearly see each day by what happens to us and to the people around us.

It's critical for us to sharpen our observation skills so that we can become more open and more objective each day — that way, it is easier for us to accept the truth. Relax and meditate!

Time...tick, tock!

My niece gave me a wall clock as a birthday gift, in one late evening. After a bit of consideration, I decided to hang the clock right above the family photo. It looks good and right in that spot.

Then suddenly, as I was walking back and forth during my walking meditation, I happened to look at the clock and realize that a deep message was hidden right there: time and family are the most important elements of our lives. Even so, spending enough time with family is a challenge for almost everyone. Due to our jobs, our daily tasks, our desires and ambitions, it seems like we never have enough time for our families and loved ones, people who play such an important role in our lives. What a paradox!

Time is the only resource that goes away and then never returns, so make it a priority to spend as much time as possible with your loved ones! There will never be enough time for your family, your parents, your spouse, your children, and your friends. We need to maximize the time we do have to live life fully and to love the people who are important to us.

It seems like we have too many reasons not to spend more time with our loved ones, which is why we need to remind ourselves that we need to prioritize our family time. Having physical reminders like my clock and my family photo and carrying reminders with us strengthens our wish to have more time with loved ones.

That said, there is another important and rather contradictory truth: we don't usually take enough time for ourselves to care for our own body and mind. That's very dangerous! We need to take time for ourselves, too, so that we can improve our own lives and be better partners, friends, family members, etc.

Happiness comes in large part from freedom, and although the first freedom we usually need to acquire in order to advance along our happiness journey is financial freedom, the second freedom we need to acquire is time, specifically how we can use our time wisely and make the most out of our relationships with the people we care about.

Impermanence

The elegant lotus blossoms and stays beautiful for two days. Then it fades and withers.
Being born. Dying. Impermanence.

We come into this world in order to go away from it in the end. No exception. Yet we only seem to see impermanence around us. We see that people are growing old and one by one are departing from this life, but we usually forget that we ourselves are also progressing during this very process.

We can't change this law of nature — this law of impermanence — so we had better be prepared to cooperate with impermanence in the best way possible. Knowing that we'll all come to an end, we should ask ourselves how we can transition into our next lives in the most meaningful way. And when we find answers to that question, we should act on them immediately. No more waiting!

I believe that we go away from this world in order to return and that how we return depends very much on the actions, thoughts, and statements that we cultivate right here and right now.

Regularly let your mind rest. Regularly feed it with silence and quietness. When you do, your body and mind will tell what you need to do. The answer lies within you, inside your body and mind, not anywhere else. You are your answer.

You can rely on yourself!

Every one of us has our own difficulties and stories that are hard to share. Often, complaining to other people about our difficulties and trying to find solutions to our problems from other people are ineffective. Books, teachers, family, and friends can help us gain new perspectives and knowledge, but ultimately, if we don't change our actions, statements, and thoughts, how can we hope to get different results? After all, everything that happens to us is the result of our past actions, thoughts, and statements.

While others may have suggestions for us, they are unlikely to have solutions. Instead, our solutions lie within our own actions, thoughts, and statements that we carry out in each present moment. That is why, as the Buddha taught, "You can rely on yourself!" Relying on yourself enables you to confidently take the next step forward in your life.

To be able to rely on yourself, you need to pay attention to your actions, statements, and thoughts and then change them accordingly in order to shape a better, brighter future for yourself. Only then will you be on the road to reaching happiness.

Peace rewarding for yourself

I had the chance to share the successful stories of my KMS Technology company with a HR community in Ho Chi Minh city. The image captured above was the most meaningful part of the event — during that session, I hosted a brief relaxation session with nearly the 300 people who were in the hall. Together, we let our minds and bodies rest and relax for ten minutes.

Take a look at everyone's calm and peaceful expressions. Although the hall was crowded, you can certainly feel peacefulness coming through the image.

The great thing is that we can always reward ourselves with peaceful moments. And we can do that at no cost even though those peaceful moments offer invaluable benefits to our lives!

All you need to do is find a quiet place where people won't bother you for ten minutes. Turn on the guided script that I've recorded and shared below, then follow whatever it tells you to do.

It's so simple and it feels so good to reward yourself with peaceful moments!

You can access to the guided script from the QR code above or the link below:

https://viethungnguyen.com/2019/01/15/hay-thu-gian-lets-relax/

United with nature!

Sometimes, once you have reached a calm mental state of pure tranquility and peace, you can feel like you're one with nature — at that moment, nature suddenly becomes closer and closer and then unites with you. You are a tree, a rock, a flower amongst nature, a place where bees and butterflies can peacefully take refuge. Those peaceful moments are invaluable and meaningful.

Alone, but not lonely

Alone!
Quiet.
And peaceful.

Alone, but not feeling lonely. Alone, but still full of balance, connected with your surroundings, in touch with loved ones.
It sounds like a paradox, but that is a real truth!

PART 2: HAPPINESS IN THE WORKPLACE

In order to survive, most of us need to go to work and earn a living. But despite that reality, when I asked the question "Are you happy to go to work?" at a conference of 200 HR experts, I got quite a few shaking heads from the crowd. But if we must work to survive, why are so many people so disappointed with their work? It shouldn't be that way. This part of the book is a collection of all my suggestions, notes, and experiences from my time working first as an employee, then as a manager, and then as a business owner. These ideas helped me develop myself, and I hope they are also sources of inspiration that others can use to be more successful at work and in life.

The Happiness Journal

Hell or heaven?

Every one of us has the same 24 hours in the day. No more, no less — time is the same for all of us. If there is something that's inherently "fair" in life, I think this is it.

Minus time for sleeping, eating, and commuting, we only have about 14 hours left in each day. And usually we spend most of that time at our office, maybe as much as ten hours per day. Hence, we can say that we spend roughly two-thirds of our time in the office with our colleagues. If you don't want to come into your workplace each day or if you don't care for your co-workers, then you are really unlucky, because you're probably spending two-thirds of your time living in what I would call hell.

I often tell my friends and my family that during the ten years I spent working at KMS, I was very lucky, because I wanted to come into the office each morning. Why? Because the office was not just work — it was also where I spent time with my co-workers who were also my friends. They were like my brothers and sisters, and I could trust them and share with them my ups and downs, successes and failures, sadness and happiness.

If you can spend two-thirds of your time with people you consider to be friends and like brothers and sisters, you can do even more meaningful things. You can gather outside of work and simply have little chit-chats. You can spend weekends doing charity trips, going out and sharing your collective knowledge and experience with others. You can share what you've learned as a company with university students. Or you can gather to celebrate Halloween or Christmas or the Lunar New Year. You will share many wonderful moments with your colleagues, and all that is because your brothers and sisters and friends are waiting for you in the office.

I was certainly fortunate to be a member of the big KMS family for a decade! I was lucky to go to work and spend my days with people I called my second family. Basically, I lived in heaven.

If you don't already live in heaven, I hope you can find that kind of workplace for yourself.

The piece of log and the Buddha statue

I found a meaningful story on YouTube that went like this: *"A big, valuable piece of log was donated to a Buddhist temple, but it was left in the backyard, gathering moisture for years. One day, the abbot invited an artist to come to the temple to make something out of the log. He carved it into a beautiful Buddha statue that was then put into the main hall. After that, everyone came to visit the temple and show their respect to the statue…which used to be just a piece of forgotten log."*

Sometimes we're like that: a forgotten piece of log. If no one "carves" us, how can we grow and develop and become something better? At work and in life, many times we receive criticism and feedback. It's not always easy to accept that. What we need to do is to keep a calm and open mind so that we can receive and think thoroughly about criticism and feedback.

If what others say is correct, we're lucky, because we've received a valuable gift. If what others say is incorrect, then we don't need to worry about it. Either way, if you can either constructively use criticism or ignore incorrect criticism, you will have grown into a more mature human being.

Many times, it's hard to handle criticism in the present moment. When that happens, you have the option to stay silent and spend more time thinking about what the other person has said before you respond. That's a meaningful PAUSE button for our lives. Use it!

And it's not just criticism and feedback that sculpts you — all of your conflicts, challenges, difficulties, suffering, and even happiness are doing the same job of shaping you into becoming a better person.

Let everyone sculpt you! And remember that even if you don't like it, people are going to keep sculpting you one way or another. You can't control that. It's also great to remind yourself that if you are sculpted by a great artist (i.e., someone who criticizes in a useful way), you will become more "beautiful" as a result!

Where does self-confidence come from?

Back when I was in my 20s, I had to ask myself one question a lot: "Where does self-confidence come from?" That was because I was not a confident person — I had a lot of worries and fears and felt like I was not ready to cope with a lot of things. Fortunately, I (eventually) found the answer, and I hope my answer also helps you if you are in that same situation.

The very first thing I learned is that no one else can make you confident. Family members can help a bit, yes, and friends can give you encouragement when you're faced with challenges and difficulties. Teachers and mentors can give you advice. But only you can give yourself self-confidence. Confidence comes from within, by looking inward and observing how your thoughts, actions, and statements impact your life.

Next, I learned that confidence is derived from going through life's ups and downs, successes and failures, bitterness and sweetness. You can learn a lot from those lessons. And you become wiser from those lessons! Those deep experiences can help relieve your fears, worries, sadness, and insecurities the next time you're faced with the same challenge. The more experiences you have, the more confidence you attain.

Start with one simple step: get to know more about yourself. What are your strengths? Your weaknesses? What is your life's purpose? What makes you happy? What job would be the most suitable for you? What can you contribute to this life, to your family, to your relatives, and to your friends? Once you have clear answers to those questions, you'll know how and where you can contribute and which situations will be challenging for you.

All of us face many difficulties and unexpected things as we go through life. And even if we have a deep understanding of ourselves, we'll realize that there are many things we don't know about in this world, many things we can't foresee and plan for in advance. Understanding and deeply feeling this truth can help us more easily accept the difficulties and challenges that are continuously thrown at us. We can accept those without blaming others or blaming ourselves. As a result, we can be more open-minded. We can reasonably choose a response that best benefits us and helps us grow into better and happier people. That's real self-confidence, right?

Self-confidence comes from deeply experiencing life's obstacles and from gaining a deeper understanding of yourself.

What do you need to deliver inspirational public talks?

I am a shy person. I'm not comfortable meeting strangers. I'm not a public speaker. Yet people often see me confidently delivering speeches in public and talking to people I don't know. How do I do that?

I do have a secret, and I'm going to unveil it here. I've realized that once I can be genuine and authentic and if I can talk about the things I'm passionate about, public speaking skills are no longer important. Because then I'm able to talk from my heart with passion and confidence and in a natural way. And that's when audiences become engaged. All I need to do then is just focus on sharing what I know deeply and what I'm passionate about.

That's the secret! I believe it will work for you as well. The key is being your true self and sharing what you really know and believe.

Peaceful mind vs. passionate pursuit

I received an email from a friend asking me if it's paradox to want to have a peaceful mind *and* simultaneously pursue one's passion. And here is my reply:

Hi there,

You should go back to the essential question of your life: what makes you happy? Assume that you have the 1.0 version of the answer and then invest your time and effort in achieving it. Once you have achieved the 1.0 version, reevaluate to see if that is making you truly happy or not. Most of the time, your happiness only lasts for a short period of time — you'll probably find another version (say, 2.0) of the answer. This is a forever-repeating process as you grow and become happier within your circle of spiritual development. Remember, you should not waste your time and effort if what you are doing doesn't bring you closer to happiness.

Life always "awards" us with many expensive lessons. Some of us are quick and deep learners; some of us are not. Once you finish one lesson, you'll get the next one, again and again.

Unfortunately, most of us don't really learn. Therefore, the same old lesson (in different forms) may keep coming at us and challenging us. Oddly, we tend to like and get addicted to whatever makes us suffer. Most people don't seriously learn life's lessons until their lives have collapsed (their marriage or finances are in trouble, they have become ill, etc.) and they're stuck and feel like there is no way out.

Because of the difficulties that you said you and your

family have had recently, you're starting to look for solutions. You want to learn. That's great!

Back to your question about can you have a peaceful mind and passionately pursue your goals at the same time? To answer that, ask yourself this question: if a particular pursuit makes your mind and life chaotic, why would you pursue it? What is more important for your life: a peaceful mind or a passionate pursuit? I think you already know the answer.

My answer is that you should pay attention to the most important thing in your life, which is attaining a peaceful mind, but you may not agree with that, at least not yet. So the simpler answer is to do whatever you want to do. But just make sure of one thing: thoroughly consider the good and bad consequences of what you want to do next. And make sure it won't harm anyone, including you. Then go for it! Directly experience and feel it for yourself.

During your journey, it's also important to observe what happens as a result of pursuing your goal and to feel the impact it has on your body and mind. That way, you'll know if what you're doing is beneficial for you (or not) so that you can cultivate "meaningful" seeds and stop planting "harmful" seeds.

Passionately pursuing your goals doesn't need to come at the expense of having a peaceful mind. For example, my passion is meditating and cultivating positive thoughts for my soul and for the people around me. The more I do this, the closer I get to having a peaceful mind. There is no conflict between the two because my passionate pursuit gives me greater peace. It's a matter of choosing wisely.

I've learned that in terms of our jobs, we should aim for

only having two purposes: earning a living (i.e., our survival) and learning / growing. If you go beyond those two reasons, be careful! Essentially, you need to observe how your job impacts your happiness journey. And your observations need to be continuous. If what you do each and every day is not aligned with your ultimate happiness, then why do you need to do more of it? That's why you need to carefully balance your job and your life direction.

Changing fate and creating luck

"Fate" and "luck" seem like they are beyond our control. However, I think we can greatly influence our own fate and our own luck. How do we do that?

We come to this world, we grow within it, and we depart from this world. That's as certain as the sun rising and setting every day. And once we depart from this world, we can't bring any tangible assets with us to the "other side." We can only leave things behind.

The most valuable things we can leave behind are not big houses or money or jewelry or even fame or reputation. I think the most valuable things we can leave behind are the relationships we've built with our families and friends and co-workers. Interestingly, those relationships are also the ones that can have a critical influence on our fate and luck during the course of our lives.

Over the last 20 years, I have had a lot of luck in my life: many great friends, great business partners, great careers. How did that happen? As best I can tell, here are a few reasons why:

- I have always tried my best to complete the jobs I was assigned. I have always finished my work to the best of my ability and before the deadline, exceeding my managers' and clients' expectations. To accomplish that, I usually focused on one thing: improving my skills by continuously reading and learning about all of the cutting-edge technologies in my field. I've also worked a lot of overtime to assure that the work would get done on time. That's how I can effectively contribute to the success of the group and the company. I think it's also the best way to promote my personal brand. My actions communicate my intentions to the people around me.

- I've been able to identify and align with people who are serious about their work and their life. It's easy to spot them in a crowd — they are the people with positive attitudes, the people who are joyful. They contribute to the success of the group in a natural and relaxed manner. They don't blame others. You can easily see their desire to advance their career and their life to the next level.
- I have learned from those people and have listened to their criticisms of me (even though it's not always easy to do that). If I found their criticism to be correct, I would work to improve myself. When their criticism was unfounded, I learned to disregard what they said and not be discouraged by them.

As a result of these actions, many people have grown to trust me. I think that is the origin of all the luck I've had.

If you do your job well and you always commit to advancing yourself at work and in life, to finding and learning from positive people, to continuously contributing to the success of the group and the people around you, then luck will surely knock on the door of your life. Luck comes from the people you have known and have worked with. Luck comes from the people who have a high level of trust in you. These people are also the biggest assets you will ever have. Can you name who they are?

Five qualities to build your success and more importantly your happiness

To enjoy a happy life, you'll need to have these five qualities: integrity, openness, self-awareness, great communication skills, and a willingness to contribute to other's successes and happiness. Let me go more into the details.

Always conduct yourself with integrity

This is absolutely not an easy thing to do! It is easy to be intimidated or overcome by negative news and scandals. Nevertheless, you must maintain your own integrity if you really want to build a solid foundation for a brighter future.

It's hard to explain what the simple word "integrity" means. For me, it's easier to remember it like this: you live in such a way that you can sleep well at night because you are living an honest and noble life, one that doesn't harm anyone, including yourself. Because you sleep well, you are refreshed and rested. Your body and mind are recharged. As the result of that, in the morning, your mind is clearer and can function with greater clarity, which means you're more mindful and can make wiser decisions. Day by day, you grow and become more mature. That's how you can advance yourself in the most meaningful way.

On the other hand, if you live in such a way that you can't get a good night's sleep due to harmful actions, thoughts, and statements, your life will gradually go downhill. Worse yet, in order to escape from your depression, you might take up addictive substances (drinking, cigarettes, drugs) that bring you nothing but more suffering and more depression. Also, with more and more of those addictive substances in your life, it's harder to cultivate a peaceful mind; gradually, your energy and mindfulness fade bit by bit, day by day. You become exhausted, both mentally and physically. That's the root of dullness in your mind. That's also the path to your life going perpetually downhill.

If you knew the ultimate results of the two options above, which one would you choose? You know the answer. If you really want to be successful and happy in a long-term and sustainable manner, commit to maintaining your integrity at all costs. That's the quickest route to happiness. And note that there is no shortcut to having integrity.

Practice and maintain having an open mind

Being open-minded is essential for surviving and growing. Why? I learned this from a Buddhist monk: *"In reality, throughout our life of being born, growing, and dying, we're very small wherever we are."* Yes, we are very tiny in this world. And that's the reason why we need to be humble — only then can we have an open attitude and listen and learn. What we know is quite limited; therefore, we need to be continuously learning.

If we have a closed mind, we can only swim around within the boundaries of our limited knowledge. More dangerously, it is harder for us to see and realize our mistakes or our weaknesses if we're too closed off from the world; it's harder for us to receive feedback and criticism. As a result, we become more and more closed-off and then can never go beyond our ever-shrinking limitations.

To attain an open mind, start by listening and observing what is happening to you and around you. Listen and observe in a relaxed way and without judgment. This includes accepting the differences around us: differences in races, differences in shapes and forms, differences in thoughts. By observing without judgment, you offer respect for those differences.

When we maintain an open, curious mindset, it's easier for us to accept life's difficulties and challenges. With that acceptance, it's easier for us to learn from those challenges and difficulties in order to grow and become more confident and stronger instead of succumbing to self-pity and blaming everything and everyone else for our difficulties.

Cultivate self-awareness

Because no individual person knows a lot, we collectively wind up having many misconceptions about ourselves and others. But we need to attain more knowledge to have a better life.

Do you know what your strengths are? How about your weaknesses? What makes you happy? What types of work or professions would be suitable for you? What do you really want to become in the next six months, twelve months, two years, five years, ten years?

What do you want people to remember about you? What are the core values that you believe in, respect, and practice daily? Are you able to control your emotions, or do your emotions usually drive you over the edge and create big issues for you, especially in terms of your relationships? Can you be yourself around other people, or do you lose your true self around other people? What is your life's purpose?

Not many of us ask these questions, but it's a good idea to think about what your answers would be. And if you pay attention to yourself and what's happening around you, you will see that your answers keep changing over time depending on your maturity level. With an open mindset, you will be able to explore and understand more about yourself and your surroundings each and every day. I'm certain that you will be surprised by what you find out! And with that understanding, you will see how you can best contribute, develop, and grow.

There's a key principle in personal development, and it's called being strength-based. It suggests that we develop ourselves by building on our strengths rather than focusing on improving our weaknesses. To do that, you need to know what your talents and strengths are. I trust that your answers will be tightly connected to what your passions are. If you want to learn more about this strength-based principle, you can refer to the book named *Strengths Finder 2.0*.

Enrich your communication skills

We communicate during every moment we are

alive. We talk to our family members, friends, and co-workers. Even when we're alone, we are still communicating — we communicate with ourselves and talk to ourselves quite a lot.

Communication is the core skill we need to work and to live. If you can't effectively express your thoughts, how can people understand what you are trying to do and then help you or give you feedback? Your communication style also helps you gain trust and respect from people around you and vice versa.

Practicing and developing communication skills is a lifelong journey, and therefore, you need to be patient and determined. Communication really starts with listening and observing in an objective manner, which is thoroughly and sensibly. Next, communication means being open to sharing your personal thoughts and viewpoints with other people. Doing so plays a very important role in assuring that people can understand what you're saying — sharing your thoughts establishes intimacy and trust between you and them. And trust is what creates the foundation of a healthy relationship, making the exchange of information between you and other people smoother and more effective.

Usually, communicating completely includes the four components below:
1. What you have observed?
2. Your thoughts and conclusions based on your knowledge and direct experience with what you observed.

3. Your resulting feelings and sensations.
4. Action steps that you and others can take to improve the situation in a positive manner that is beneficial for all parties. That should be the ultimate goal of any conversation or communication, right?

I learned these ideas from a book called ***How to Communicate: The Ultimate Guide to Improving Your Personal and Professional Relationships***. You can find a lot more information there.

Self-communicating is very important, too! After all, we spend most of our time talking to ourselves. To maintain a positive and flexible self, you need to be honest, open, and true to yourself, and you need to communicate with yourself in a positive manner.

Always be a contributor

Societies, families, and companies all really need people who can contribute. Only people who contribute can energize projects as well as people and only people who contribute can create successes and meaningful achievements.

I love this teaching from a Buddhist monk: "*Completely be in whatever you can do to contribute, in whatever you can learn to contribute, in whatever responsibility you can take to contribute. Never stop changing. That's the best way to find out what your own self is.*" Yes! That is so true. In order to become a contributor, you need to be positive, open-minded, willing to take charge, and willing to overcome many difficulties and challenges without getting discouraged or blaming others.

More often than not, life is not what we expected. If we're facing any difficulties or challenges, we should ask "How can I contribute to solving this challenge?" rather than "Why can't I be fortunate like others are?" or "Why do so many road blocks keep popping up in front of me?" An insightful question can lead you to the correct solution. In this case, it will help you become a contributor instead of a destroyer.

Maintaining the attitude of a contributor means you won't hesitate to finish tasks that people usually don't want to do (i.e., chores, errands, assorted tedious but necessary tasks). By striving to truly contribute, you'll actively seek new, creative approaches to solving problems instead of just following the same old path.

Once you are 100% wholeheartedly putting your efforts into contributing, something magical happens: you'll gain the ability to focus without looking around and comparing what you're doing to what others are doing. Due to this focus, you can learn a lot as well as grow a lot. That is the award you give yourself that you don't need anyone else to grant you. Even if the final results are not what you expected, your 100% efforts to contribute will clearly demonstrate your value to the company and to the people around you. This is how you gain more trust from your co-workers and bosses. Being trusted by those around you is how you can change your fate and then create your own fortune, your own luck.

If you are patient and persistent in practicing

integrity and openness, if you continuously seek to gain a deeper understanding of yourself, if you continuously practice and improve your communication skills and keep contributing, you will reap success in your career and in your life. And that success will bring you happiness and fulfillment in this world.

The word "family"

When I was being filmed as part of a video about KMS Technology, I was asked to use one word to describe what I liked the most about KMS. Immediately, I popped out the word "family." And also immediately, the guy filming me said, "Can you pick another word?"

A little bit embarrassed and disappointed, I told him, "I co-founded the company about nine years ago, and now I cannot pick a word for KMS — for me, it is all about family. And friendship."

"Friendship... Can you use that word?" suggested the guy. I agreed to say that word two or three times so that we could finish filming the segment, but I kept in mind that I really wanted to say the word "family" because it was the most important thing about KMS to me.

Later on, I found out the reason why I could not use the word "family" — it was simply because many other people had used that exact same word before me, leaving me no option to repeat it in the video. I was so thrilled to know that. What a wonderful reason for that word having been rejected!

I once heard a meaningful quote: *"Choose a job you love, and you will never have to work a day in your life."* How very true!

If you can find your family at work, your second family, I'm certain that then you'll have a job you love. And you won't have to work a day after that.

So, if your current company is not your second family, find one! Move on and find your family somewhere else. If you can't look for another job, think about how you could contribute to building a second family at your current company. That needs to start with you! Start building your family within your group. Don't wait for your CEO to do that! (They may not do it, anyway.)

Also note that you can't expect someone else to build your family for you if you're not contributing. You need to be part of it and act upon it in order to build your second family at work. Once you have, you'll experience more happiness and fulfillment when you come to your workplace each and every day.

Are you proud of what you are doing?

During my trip to the US in early December 2016, I had a chance to dine in a 176-year-old restaurant. What an impressive history! The restaurant is a family-run business that has been managed by five or six generations. The food was great, and I liked it a lot — plenty of fresh and delicious seafood served in a warm, welcoming environment.

I wasn't surprised that the food was good, actually, but I was surprised by something else that came to my attention when the waiter told us about the restaurant and what they are proud of. As he spoke, his voice was full of energy, talking about the food, the restaurant itself, and his recommendations for us regarding the evening's menu choices. You couldn't miss the passion in his voice.

And I couldn't help but to be addicted to his passion. I couldn't help but to ask him if I could take a picture with him. The restaurant was great and the food was great, but he added the last piece of the puzzle and made it a completely beautiful night, a complete experience. And why was that?

From his energy, I could feel his pride for the restaurant, for the great food and service the restaurant offers as well as the legacy they have built over the past 176 years. I could feel that he was very proud of the work he was doing. His pride sparked a fire within me that night, because once more, it confirmed that if you are passionate about what you are doing, you will do it well. Not only that, your passion will sweep away depression and fatigue even if you have to spend long hours working through whatever you need to work on. And interestingly, passion is contagious. During that evening, I just had to stand up, take a picture with the guy, and let him know that his passion had gotten to me.

Does your work fill you with passion or not? Are you proud of what you're doing or not? Are you proud of the company you are working for or not?

If you're not, I challenge you to fix that. Either work with yourself to find your passion or find another company where you can really align your passion with the work you do. Most of the time, that will require you to change: change your attitude, change your thoughts. Everything starts with you, not with the company.

I hope you can be happily smiling at your work like the waiter I was lucky to meet that day! And remember that your happy smiles can greatly influence the people around you as well.

Higher positions, attachments, greed, and how to deal with it all

After I had shared some suggestions on my blog about how to deal with stress, I got some interesting questions from one of my staff that I want to share with you here. These are not easy to answer for anyone, I would say. And while some answers may work for one person, they may not work for another person. Here's the first question:

"I have always believed that to achieve magical things in life, we always have to set higher standards for ourselves and try our best to achieve those. I think you would agree with me on this point."

The more I grow, the more I realize that while setting crazy goals can help us focus, people are usually confused between "correct" (meaning realistic) goals and unrealistic goals. In order to set a correct goal, you need to have enough wisdom to see it. Yet at the same time, wisdom doesn't just come from knowledge and thinking. In fact, it mostly comes from *doing*, from directly experiencing things through both failures and successes. Therefore, at first, you usually don't know what the right goal is, and consequently, you usually choose unrealistic goals.

However, you learn a lot from failing to reach those goals, and you become better at setting more realistic goals the next time. If you can realize what those failures, false expectations and disappointments mean, you can learn and grow a lot. On the other hand, if you *don't* perceive those as lessons, you'll feel a lot of stress. But if you can accept those lessons, learn from them, and do better the next time, stress won't be such a persistent part of your life.

"Do you know what the limitations of human greed should be?"

I would say that greed doesn't bring you long-term or sustainable happiness. What greed mostly does is pollute your mind. So what are the limitations? Greed itself is the limitation.

"When I am promoted at work, I always feel tired and like I have to 'protect' my higher position. What should I do?"

It is purely your choice to protect your position or not. If you choose to protect it, you'll feel a lot of pressure. And quite frankly, it's not necessary to do so. You're thinking about protecting it because you're attached to it, but truthfully, our positions in life are very temporary — a CEO today can become a prisoner tomorrow. What's the point in being attached to a position? Also, a work position is certainly not the root of happiness in life, so why do you want to attach yourself so dearly to your position that you feel you must protect it? I don't believe that is a wise thing to do.

I think the better question to ask is, "How can I best fulfill the tasks that the position entails and at the same time maintain great relationships with my co-workers, clients, and family?" I would challenge you to ask *that* question instead of wondering how you can "protect" your position. While the modified question can still give you pressure and stress, it would help you live a more meaningful life.

"Whenever we get a chance to attain a higher level, a new position, should we take it?"

We may need to seek out new positions and responsibilities depending on available opportunities and our capabilities at the time. And if you can contribute better and if it doesn't harm anybody (including yourself) to take a higher position, then why not do so? Be sure to keep asking one question, though, and that is, "What is the purpose of taking on more responsibilities?" If it is to satisfy greed or your desire for fame, you may want to think twice about what you're about to take on. But if your purpose is to positively contribute more to the happiness of the people around you, including you, then why not? Certainly, if that is your purpose, then you will know what to do next.

"Do you believe there's a real-life Forrest Gump?"

I liked *Forrest Gump* a lot — I have watched it many times. I don't remember all of the details right now, but I do remember the pure, true, unconditional love that Forrest had for his wife and his daughter. With that kind of true love in your life, everything is possible.

A final thought about all of this: I live my life in a very simple way and don't aim for any "magical things" in life. That may not help me become someone like Steve Jobs, but I'm happy with not being another

Steve Jobs. I'm happy with my own journey toward happiness and with my own spiritual development. That's more important to me, I would say. What's important to you?

A question about respect?

During one session of the leadership development program at my company, KMS, I got an interesting question from a staff member. I was the managing director of the company at that time. The question went like this: "I observed that you have a tendency to be close to your staff. Aren't you afraid that one day, once you've gotten too close to them, people will lose respect for you?"

Wow, that was one of the best questions I got during training!

If I had gotten that question about eight or ten years previously, I don't think I would have been comfortable handling it. But by the time I *did* get the question, I had come to believe that being close to co-workers was what I should do, no matter what position I held at the company (or at any company in the future). I could also see why some people might worry about doing that. In fact, considering that I was the top guy of a 500-person organization, it seemed like there could indeed be more to worry about — the traditional Asian culture in Vietnam promotes having gaps between managers and subordinates, so some people might think it could do more harm than good to be close to staff. If the relationship became too close, would that be a bad thing? Would I indeed lose the respect of my co-workers?

Here is how I replied to that question: "People respect me because of what I can do for them and how

I can support them, because of the added value I provide for them and for the team. I would only lose respect from my co-workers if I couldn't fulfill my job of contributing, supporting, and adding value. Being close to my staff isn't a factor when it comes to me losing respect from my staff."

This is actually an excellent principle in terms of developing your leadership capability. Leadership doesn't come from your position — it comes from what you can do for the people around you. Position alone can't give you the power to be a leader. If you can greatly help and support the people around you, they will love you. They will respect you. And absolutely, they will consider you to be their leader.

So if you really want to be respected by others, the key is giving, contributing, supporting, helping, and adding value. Never stop learning and advancing yourself every day. Pick an insightful book and read it, learn from it and make positive changes. Get to know outstanding people and be inspired by them. Do something to help the people around you: start with your loved ones, then your friends, and then your community.

An ideally happy job

During lunch with one of my friends, we talked about what an ideally happy job would be. After all, if we never ask questions, we never find answers, and that's a great question! So, what is an ideally happy job?

For me, the answer is simple. It must be a job that makes you look forward to going to work when you wake up each and every morning. It is a job that you don't complain about, even if you have to spend extra time finishing your tasks. Even if you work long hours at this job, you should still be in good health, because your work should be more about entertaining you than exhausting you.

But what really is an ideally happy job? I would say it should involve two attributes: contributing and learning.

Contributing

An ideally happy job is a job that lets you really contribute at work. If you come to the office and work throughout the day, yet at the end of the day, you find out that your sweat and effort don't really help your company, neither you nor your clients are going to be happy. Or maybe you work like hell on a project only to find out that that is not what your customer wants. You feel useless, right? And then you would be demotivated, because you've realized that you have completely wasted your time.

But it could be worse. What if you come into the

office and you don't even try to do *anything*? Instead, you delay your tasks and argue with your co-workers. Again, you feel as though it's all a waste of your time. You feel unsatisfied and exhausted every day. And that's how your life starts going downhill.

Now imagine that you come into the office and work throughout the day and enjoy your work a lot. You receive compliments about the great quality of the products you have produced. You see that your co-workers love what you do, and together, you create a great service or product for your customers. You feel great not because of the achievement itself, but because you have a meaningful sense of having contributed.

If you can contribute at work, you'll find that you have a happy job. Note that in order for you to contribute, besides investing your effort, you also need to be in the right culture and the right environment and working with the right people. If your workplace has a negative culture or environment, it will be harder for you to contribute, so hard that you will eventually give up trying. This is an important note for employers, I would say! If an employer doesn't create a supportive and positive culture and environment, it's much harder for employees to contribute.

Learning

Assuming that you can contribute at work every day and you enjoy your days at work, then I would add one more attribute to the ideally happy job, and that is the ability for you to learn new things at work and to advance yourself more and more every day. This is actually a basic need of human beings: to evolve. If you don't see yourself improving after a while, you can become demotivated. While being able to contribute can keep you feeling great for a long time, eventually, you will become bored if you don't think you will learn more at work. You would feel like you are becoming obsolete. And I don't mean that you need to climb to a higher position on the corporate ladder or earn a higher salary. Instead, I mean you need to be able to gain more knowledge and more experience at work. For instance, you might learn in these ways:

- You become more of an expert in your field; for example, you become a world-class software developer or tester.
- You gain more industry-wide knowledge through what you do (banking, finance, healthcare, education, etc.).
- You learn a lot more about how to deal with people (who are always the hardest-to-deal-with living beings).

Knowing that you are learning every day will give you a great feeling. And that is happiness.

So now you can see if you currently have an ideally happy job or not by simply answering this question: *Can I be both a contributor and a learner at work?*

If not, you will need to answer the next question: *How can I be a contributor and a learner at work?*

If you can't figure out an answer to the latter

question over the next six to twelve months, you may want to find another job. And if you're an employer, these two attributes — being able to contribute and being able to learn — are important for you, too. If employers don't create jobs and environments that provide opportunities for employees to contribute and learn, it shouldn't be a surprise when people are not effective within organizations. And it shouldn't be a surprise when they leave, either.

Becoming a great manager

How to become a great manager is a hot topic for almost anyone as they move along their career path. After you graduate from university, it takes a while to be promoted to manager. That's certainly a big milestone in your career! It is also a big challenge in your career.

Remember that becoming a great manager starts from you, not anywhere else. And while you won't become a great manager overnight, if you stay focused on the journey, you will get there eventually. Here are the five basic principles that managers should consider and practice so that they can thrive in their career path.

1. **Manage yourself.** This is the first and most important thing to do. The best way to manage yourself is to never stop growing! Have high expectations of yourself and stay disciplined so that you fulfill those expectations each and every day.
2. **Master your people skills.** Great managers need to possess great people skills in order to effectively work with and lead others. Ask yourself, "How will I work with others? How will I inspire my team? How will I help them with their career development?" Knowing the answers to these questions is essential for great managers and requires a lot of commitment and effort.
3. **Execution, execution, and execution.** Actions

speak louder than words, and your actions can speak for themselves. Take ownership of your tasks, set deadlines, commit to them, and get the work done. Before making promises, understand the situation thoroughly and know how you can best contribute within the given context. Get the necessary support and help from other people or other teams who complement your and your team's weaknesses. Always act with integrity. And never, ever, blame others when you fall short (This is the hardest principle to follow, I would say).

4. **Communication is the key to success.** As a manager, you become the middleman, standing between your staff and the company. Your job is to assure that information can travel back and forth with accuracy. It means that you need to be a good listener, listening to every detail and communicating them upwards with accuracy and vice versa. And being a good listener doesn't just get the work done more effectively, it's also critical for creating trust between you and all of the team members you work with.

5. **Optimism is the best approach.** Optimists accept reality, whatever that may be. Interestingly, they may view the reality they see through a very different lens than most of the crowd. That's how they can come up with different, fresh, new ideas to solve the same problems. By being open-minded, respectful,

and caring, great managers can figure out solutions to almost any problem and can turn the process into a positive experience.

If you are already a manager, I hope this is a nice review of what you can do to grow even more! And if you're a manager-to-be, these are good skills for you to develop in order to help you get that promotion one day.

What makes a band so powerful?

I had a special experience when I was at a café one night where there was a band playing. It was so pleasant to hear them play and sing familiar songs with relaxing rhythms and lyrics! As I was enjoying all of that, suddenly, I realized a few beautiful lessons. What makes a band so powerful?

- **Passion.** If you ever watch a band playing, you'll see that they close their eyes while their hands and bodies naturally follow the rhythms and the music. You can't miss the passion that is reflected through their bodies and their moves. They act like nothing else matters except the music. When you're with your "band" of co-workers, it would be amazing to experience a similar setting, one in which everyone shares the same interests and the same desires and everyone works wholeheartedly from that place of passion.
- **Teamwork.** If you were to remove any one member of the band, I don't think the remaining members could put on such a beautiful performance. The drummer, the pianist, the bass guitarist, the lead guitarist, the vocalist... they all have their own roles in the song, and if any of them were missing, that absence would lessen the beauty of the music. They complement each other and have one and only one objective: to play a beautiful song. The

exact same thing is true for a team working together to produce beautiful outcomes. It is not the superhero in the team who makes it happen — it is the super *team* in which all members combine their skills and complement their strengths so that together, everyone can be successful.
- **Discipline.** Usually, artists like musicians are stereotyped as being not well organized, yet once they come together to play a song, they are very disciplined and cohesive. Each of them needs to be perfectly accurate in every beat of the music. If any single one of them can't be that perfectly accurate, the band cannot create a song, let alone a beautiful song. The same principle holds true for a great team.

All of these thoughts came together at the café that night. I realized that life is simple, with just a few core principles that need to be followed. You can find those principles at work and just about anywhere in your daily life. The challenge is whether you can see them or not! The good news is that once you've experienced more of life's ups and downs, you'll become more and more aware of these basic principles.

Do you see these three principles — passion, teamwork, and discipline — in your "band" at work? If you don't, work more closely with your team so that you can all play a beautiful song together. That's the best way to contribute to the success of your company.

Five things I learned from my entrepreneurial journey

Nowadays, startup companies are bursting out in every corner of the world, founded by people who have the desire and ambition to create something big, something new, something that they can look back at and be proud of. These startup founders want to contribute to the growth and development of society.

However, not every startup makes it. In his book *The E-Myth: Why Most Small Business Don't Work and What To Do About It* by *Michael E. Gerber*, the author discusses the statistics of startup businesses in America. Among one million new startups each year, after the first year, at least 40% of them are out of business. In five years, more than 80%, go bankrupt. And after five more years, more than 80% of the companies that managed to survive the first five years go out of business.

That means that only 4% of startups survive past the ten-year mark. And of course, much fewer are still in business after 20 years. As an entrepreneur, does this make you feel like you want to stop pursuing your startup? If your answer is no, keep reading!

I would love to share with you five things that I have learned from my entrepreneurial journey so far. The biggest startup project I've ever gotten involved with is KMS Technology. I co-founded the company in late 2008, and now it has more than 500 staff who specialize in providing software application development services to the US market from its development center located in Ho Chi Minh city, Vietnam. If you're struggling with your startup, I do hope my suggestions are useful for your journey.

(1) Idea or implementation: which one is more important?

Not long ago, I heard a story like this: A young man met a successful entrepreneur and wanted to share his million-dollar idea with the entrepreneur, who himself was already a millionaire. The millionaire laughed and said that he didn't want to hear about the young man's idea, saying that it's hard to tell if an idea is worth $1 million or $100 million, because either way, it is just an idea. In the Internet age, the millionaire said, ideas are everywhere.

Every startup starts with an idea, of course, but whether or not the startup can successfully turn the idea into sellable products or services is the dividing line between success and failure. And if we're talking about implementation or execution, the key is on the people side — a successful startup needs a group of people who have enough patience, persistence, and clarity to find a suitable approach as well as carry out that plan to successfully turn an idea into sellable products or services. It's the people who make it happen, not the idea or the strategy.

I don't mean to say that having an idea is not important, but you need to remember that an idea is just part of a startup's story. Once you have an idea, you need to successfully implement your idea ASAP.

Otherwise, someone else will be quicker than you, and your road to success will become a lot more difficult. Nowadays, getting to market / the speed of implementation is critical for success. And you alone can't make that happen — you need a group of partners in order to implement the idea, the strategy, and more importantly the startup dream. Having the right partners is critical to the success of your startup. So how do you pick good partners? That comes next.

(2) Superman vs. super team

Many successful startups and entrepreneurs are attached to a key person. Normally, that's the CEO of the company. This creates a misconception that the success of the company should be mainly credited to the CEO — it's like he / she is the superman or superwoman who virtually knows everything and can do everything. In my opinion, however, that's not a correct perception. Maybe the shadow of Steve Jobs is huge at Apple, but if it weren't for people like Jonathan Ivy and many others, there would not be super successful products like the MacBook Air and the iPhone. So what was the role of Mr. Jobs? His role was having the discipline and the determination to implement his vision. He was a genius, certainly. However, if he had worked entirely on his own, he could not have created wildly appealing and successful products.

In my opinion, at Apple, each person contributes to the success of those super products. Those products were created by **the right "collection" of the right**

people at **the right time**. They are the sum of everyone's efforts, not the efforts of only one superman.

This thought of mine was confirmed by Gallup research that was detailed in the books *Strengths-Finder 2.0* and *Strengths-Based Leadership*. Strengths-based leadership is an approach to personal development as well as leadership development. It points out that there is no such a superman — rather, each of us has a few strengths and many weaknesses. I think that's how and why each of us is unique.

The strengths-based approach suggests that we should focus on and maximize our contributions through utilizing our strengths, not through improving our weaknesses. Also, people succeed and thrive when they're in their strength zone, not the opposite. Therefore, if we spend a lot of time focusing on improving our weaknesses, we won't have time to invest in and develop our strengths. That means we would miss many opportunities to contribute our best toward the success of the team. Even worse, on an individual level, we would be demotivated and exhausted.

This approach also suggests building a super team of individuals with complementary strengths. That's much more practical and more effective. Also, that's the best formula for establishing a solid foundation for a startup as well as for long-lasting, sustainable teams and companies. It's similar to a basketball team. The team will need a full set of players with different skills: a center, two guards, and two forwards. Likewise, that's the best approach toward building super teams. That's all we need — the super team takes care of the rest.

For your startup business, you'll need to gather a team where each member complements the other members' strengths. And the team should have one urge in common: to seriously to create a startup. You need to start this process right now if you haven't done so yet. It usually takes a while to find suitable members for your super team. And this needs to be a continuous effort, because you will likely never have enough human resources for your team. Go out and develop your social network! Find ways to positively expand your relationships. After you've spent a while developing your network of relationships, you will start seeing the impact. If you're still hesitant, refer to my presentation _Social Networking: Why and How_ to find out how to drum up the courage to do it. You can view the presentation by scanning the QR code below:

In brief, you need to learn what your own strengths and weaknesses are. You need to continuously search for and recruit team members who complement each other's strengths in order to build a super team. That's the best approach to take if you want to have a successful startup and build a solid, long-term foundation for your company. This holds true not just during your startup phase, but for the lifetime of the company as well.

(3) Have an in-depth understanding of financial models

This is a great lesson I learned from my CEO! In order to be successful and to effectively "diagnose" company's issues — especially in the startup phase — you need to acquire an in-depth understanding of the essential financial models used to operate a business. Through these models, you can foresee quite a few issues that may happen in the near future as well as spot any hidden / potential risks and issues. Financial models include P&L models, cash-flow models, revenue models, cost-structure models, etc.

Of these models, you need to pay special attention to the cash-flow model. In any business, cash flow can be considered to be its main artery. As you can imagine, if the blood stops running through your arteries, you die, no matter how big your body is. In the cash-flow model, cash must always be positive. Any time it is zero or negative, it means that blood is no longer flowing through the "artery." And if that happens, then your business is clinically "dead." No matter how big and how strong your business is, it will stop functioning once blood can't flow through its main artery.

Not all entrepreneurs have a solid financial background; many, in fact, have limited knowledge of finances. Yet to be successful in any startup project or business, you must find ways to become knowledgeable about finance and how to use financial models in your daily operations. Doing so is critical to your success.

If you are the CEO of your startup, you should closely monitor the cash-flow model. You may even need to build your own model using a simple tool like MS Excel. You must maintain and update it weekly — if not daily — in order to have a clear forecast of your cash flow over the next three to six months. Any time the model predicts a potential issue coming up (i.e., not having a positive cash flow), you need to act on it *immediately* so that no potential issue has the chance to pop up six months down the road.

(4) Aim for a longer-term vision and mission

From the book ***Build to Last***, I learned that very few companies last longer than 50 years. That statistic may make you think that it's not necessary to build a company meant to exist for more than 50 years — after all, it's mostly not doable, right? Wrong. I urge you to think otherwise.

If you pursue a short-term vision and your mission is not big enough, you will risk getting stuck and not having any way to grow and make your company into a successful business, because you will have the tendency to stick to short-term and in-the-moment issues and you won't have any plan to move your business forward. On the other hand, having a long-term vision and mission serves as positive guidance and plays a critical role in shaping the operations of your business.

For example, the KMS mission is to contribute to the growth of the software development industry in Vietnam by continuously building and developing the next outstanding generation of software developers and software testers. This is a really challenging mission! From the beginning, I knew it would take at least ten to twenty years to see some concrete results. Even more challenging, while working on a mission, a company also needs to make sure that its business performance and its finances are in good shape.

I believe that the key to having a successful, sustainable business lies within the word "people." The KMS mission guided the company toward pursuing a few concrete actions:

- Being strict with our selection and recruitment.
- Continuously improving our program to train and build our staff, from the entry level to the management / strategic level or technical expert level.
- Especially focusing on creating opportunities for young people and the next generation.
- Continuously creating suitable opportunities that allowed our people to address challenging business problems, therefore helping our staff develop additional skills and competencies.

Once a company has committed to this kind of long-term mission, it's easy to identify what to do next.

I completely believe in the importance of having a

long-term vision and mission. I encourage startup founders and entrepreneurs to establish / envision long-term visions and missions. Both are important steps to gaining clarity during the startup journey. Remember, you're in it for the long haul!

(5) No matter what the end result is, you will grow a LOT during your startup journey

Before founding a startup, most of us usually have to consider many perspectives. What are the risks? What are your family responsibilities? Do you have a fear of failure? Might you lose face with friends and family if you fail?

To fill in more of the picture, no matter how great your idea is and how good your plan is, there is no 100% guarantee that your startup will be a success. There are always risks. There is always the chance that things will not play out as expected. And at the same time, events change each and every moment, adding more complications to your startup journey. Honestly, you can't be certain about anything. Plus, as previously mentioned, only about 4% of startups make it past the ten-year mark. So given all of those hard truths, should you stick with your startup idea?

Founding a startup only makes sense for those who have the passion to do so — it isn't an appropriate idea for everybody. That said, while financial success is the ultimate goal of any startup, I don't think it's the biggest achievement that a founder can attain during the startup journey. No, the biggest reward is the experience that entrepreneurs have to go through during the course of their journeys.

There are lessons that no schools can teach. Once you are in the position of being the decision-maker and are steering your startup, you will become a lot more mature. You'll encounter many challenges along the startup journey: managing yourself, managing and operating your business through vertical functions like HR, business strategies, marketing, sales, finance, customer services… I think the lessons you gain from having those experiences are the most valuable achievements of the startup journey, no matter if the startup is successful or not.

Conclusion

If you're still reading this, I hope that means you have startup blood running in your veins. If you do, you need to start doing something about it!

Human resources are always the key element of any successful startup / company, so begin your journey by extending your social network. Meet others and recruit people who have the same startup desires that you have and who believe in the same principles about doing business and living this life. It's critical to find those who can complement your weaknesses so that you can build a super team. Good luck!

PART 3: SEEKING YOUR OWN TRUTHFUL HAPPINESS

We and not anyone else are responsible for our own lives. Happiness or suffering lies within our hands! This is the ultimate freedom that the Buddha kept teaching us right up until the day he departed from this world.

The Happiness Journal

Two questions for your life

Continuously ask yourself these two questions: (1) What would make you happy? and (2) How would you want to live your life today, in one more year, in five more years, and once you're 80?

Many of us blindly follow the inertia of our cultures, our traditions, and our customs whether we're aware of it or not. I don't think that's truly living — I think real living is to live for ourselves and to be ourselves. If we don't live for ourselves and can't be our true selves, it's like we're only chasing a shadow of happiness, not the real thing. What would make you happy? Start your true life journey by asking that question.

Once you have the answer, the next step is to validate the answer, to see if fulfilling the answer can bring you happiness. You'll probably change a lot during this process.

The interesting thing is that 99.99% of the time, after you've achieved what you think would make you happy, you realize that you're not truly happy yet and that you need to revise your answer. You start the validation process again. And you change again. This process is not chasing the shadow — rather, it's the spiraling evolutionary process of maturing, and that's a wonderful thing.

We need to directly answer our questions about what brings us happiness, and we need to feel those answers in our body and mind. No one can answer for us. But whatever we do, we must remember not to harm anyone, including ourselves. Many people often talk about saving the world, but sadly, they can't save themselves. If you don't have the answers to your own life, how can you know what the answers are for others?

If you can deeply sense what is happening in your body and mind, you can see and learn a lot about what you need to do. The interesting thing is that you don't need to go anywhere to learn these answers. Nowhere else! Just be in the here and now — the answers are right inside your body and mind.

Your heart hurts if you do something that harms someone else or yourself. Your heart doesn't lie about that. The challenge is to really sense and listen to your inner voice, which not many people do. But really, you only need to continuously observe your heart and yourself. From there, you'll guide yourself to finding what makes you happy. That's the whole reason why practicing self-observation (and meditating) can help you advance to a better life.

It is important to note that being able to accept the reality of whatever has happened to us is what enables us to start seeing our way out of difficulties. If we accept our situations, we can go beyond the label of "good" or "bad" that we've stuck to whatever has happened. From there, it's easier for us to try to do whatever is within our control to improve the situation instead of blaming others and feeling pity for ourselves. We don't need to move mountains to deal with our challenges! All we need is to apply clarity, integrity, ethics, and wisdom to each of our actions. *That's* what helps us deal with our daily difficulties. Of course, that's more easily said than done.

Before we can help anybody else pursue their happiness, we need to know how to pursue and achieve our own. Unfortunately, many people don't take responsibility for their own happiness, and that's the origin of "bad luck" for us and for the people around us.

If we are seriously honest with ourselves, if we truly respect ourselves and seriously seek our own happiness, then our actions, statements, and thoughts will naturally send meaningful and much-needed messages out to the world. Doing that also gives us and others courage and positively influences the people around us. What a wonderful way to be!

What is happiness?

I believe that the deepest desire we all have is to seek our own happiness. I am no exception. For me, however, happiness is a lifetime journey, not just a destination. I'd like to share some thoughts I've had about happiness as I'm about halfway through my life journey.

The key to happiness, I think, is quite simple: deeply understand your true self. That will guide you to happiness. Understanding your true self heals and resolves conflicts and difficulties within your existing relationships. This is a very simple concept, but it isn't an easy one. Self-understanding requires a lot of belief, determination, patience, and discipline. It's hard! Yet it's worth every metaphorical penny you spend on it.

I sense and get closer to my happiness each day, I can feel it! No words can completely describe the process, but I can share a few perspectives with you:

- I am happy once I can be myself. If I can be myself, I will have a lot of confidence, tranquility, and calmness even though difficulties and challenges will keep coming my way.
- I am happy that I don't have to force myself to be a different person because of any pressure from the people around me (my family, my community, etc.).
- I don't derive happiness from people doing what I want them to do, nor does happiness come

from fulfilling my own stubborn or selfish satisfactions. Happiness isn't something that stems from only benefitting ourselves and not caring if the people around us are benefitting or not.
- Happiness means respecting your right to be happy as well as the right of others to be happy. That kind of happiness means that while you need to persist in following your own path to happiness, you can keep your heart open to helping and supporting others as they pursue their own happiness, even if their path is much different than yours.

Once you can have that kind of happiness, you can be a source of happiness and motivation for your loved ones and the people around you. True happiness is built upon kindness and an open heart.

Of course, you won't gain an in-depth understanding of yourself overnight. That's not realistic. Understanding yourself is a lifelong journey. And it continues in your next life, too, if you believe in reincarnation like I do. You will know a little bit more about yourself each day. Gradually, the longer you seek understanding, the more confidence you will gain and the more positivity you will have.

I started my happiness pursuit journey around ten years ago, and the longer I've been on this journey, the closer I have become to my true self. I no longer complain about who I am.

I hope you will join me in pursuing your own journey to happiness! Just start by investing your time and effort in getting know more about yourself.

Things change, anyway

Whether you want this or not, whether you believe it or not, the version of you today is always different from the version of you yesterday. It doesn't take New Year's Day to change yourself — you've already been changing each and every second!

Seeing as this process is inevitable, choose who the new you is and choose to make meaningful changes in your life. Change for the better! Change to be happier. Change to be more loving and more kind.

Sure, saying "Happy New Year!" is a great reminder to look back and change, but you don't need to wait until New Year's to heed those reminders. You can change now, in this present moment. Don't wait to hear "Happy New Year"! Make positive changes *now*.

Two wolves

I learned this meaningful story from a tale told by the Cherokee people.

Image source: HTTPS://WOLVESONLINE.COM/TAG/BREEDING-PAIR/

An old Cherokee is teaching his grandson about life. "A fight is going on inside me," he says to the boy. "It is a terrible fight, and it is between two wolves. One is evil: he is anger, envy, sorrow, regret, greed, arrogance, self-pity, guilt, resentment, inferiority, lies, false pride, superiority, and ego. The other is good: he is joy, peace, love, hope, serenity, humility, kindness, benevolence, empathy, generosity, truth, compassion, and faith. The same fight is going on inside you — and inside every other person, too."

The grandson thinks about this for a minute and then asks his grandfather, "Which wolf will win?"

The old Cherokee simply replies, "The one you feed."

This is so true! We can't blame anyone else for our suffering. It's critical to understand that the origin of whatever we get in this world really is derived from "the food for our soul" that we feed to our mind every day. That food determines what we deserve in life at the present moment as well as in the future. Which wolf are you feeding?

Maintain good health

Total health consists of two essential parts: physical health and mental health. These two mutually support and complement each other. A person with great physical health usually maintains great mental health and vice versa. Especially as we grow older, we should be more focused on both of these aspects of health.

Eat right

There is an old Vietnamese saying that goes like this: "Problems come from the mouth." So true! If you don't use proper words when talking to others (or even to yourself), you will wind up with problems. But there could be another meaning behind this phrase, namely potential health issues that are a result of our daily eating habits, which also pass through our mouths. We have the tendency to eat more than our body really needs, and many of our health issues are a direct consequence of our desire to eat more delicious food.

One way to deal with this tendency is to learn about what your body needs and then put together a customized eating program for your particular needs and lifestyle. Work with health professionals and map out a plan as soon as you can — that's a great way to prevent many health issues from ever happening.

My plan is doing what the Japanese recommend: only eat until you're 80% full. For lunch or dinner, I usually only have one small bowl of rice, and before having rice, I usually try to fill up with as many vegetables as I can. I'm in pretty good shape at the age of 41, and it's mainly because of this eating habit. I joke that because I'm too lazy to exercise, I have to maintain a good balance by eating less. I think that's a good strategy.

Regularly exercise

While what you eat plays a very important role in your physical health that you should not ignore, to maintain great physical health, you also have to exercise. You don't need to get involved in expensive sports — exercise can be anything. Just remember this rule: exercise at least three times a week for 30 to 60 minutes each time, and you need to sweat during the session.

Each of us needs to choose exercise that's suitable. I have learned that competitive sports don't work for me, so instead, I do things like swim, yoga, and tai chi, because those *do* suit my style.

Mentally exercise and strengthen your mind

Lots of people make sure to get physical exercise, but often, we are too busy to have time to care about our mental health. Not exercising mentally is even more dangerous than not exercising physically, I would say, partly because many people are depressed in our modern world. If you skip exercising your mind, your mind will gradually be exhausted by all of your stresses, worries, and fears. And once your mind has become weak, it can cause physical diseases: stomach issues, liver issues, heart issues, immune issues, you name it. So while depression starts in your mind, eventually, it can turn into a critical physical health issue before you even know it. Be careful!

Because our muscles can get lazy if we let them, we need to stretch through physical exercises to make our muscles strong. But we can't apply the same principle to mental health — we can't give our minds more work. Our minds already have too many things running around inside of them! Most of the time, we can't *stop* our minds from thinking. Therefore, in order to refresh, recharge, and renew our minds, we need a lot of rest and relaxation. After all, after intensive physical exercise, you need to let your muscles rest, because otherwise, you'll be physically exhausted. Our mind is like a tired muscle after it has continuously undergone intensive exercise. The main goal of mentally exercising is to let the mind rest and relax on a regular basis.

One way to do that is to spend time on hobbies, like painting, playing instruments, or cooking. Meditation has also proven to be an effective option for relaxing the mind. It's a very powerful option, I would say.

As is the case with physical exercise, you need to choose a good mental exercise for yourself. To improve my mental health, I mostly meditate for this purpose, and I've seen results that go beyond mental health improvements — meditation has granted me more and more wisdom and therefore happiness, too.

In brief, your total health consists of two parts: your physical health and your mental health. If you understand that both halves are equally important and you regularly exercise your body and your mind — plus you monitor and control what you eat — then you can avoid most health issues. And remember, "exercising" the mind means letting it relax!

How to gain self-confidence

This is from a speech I prepared for a KMS Toastmasters Club gathering. I think it's worth sharing here.

Fear often makes us lose our self-confidence: we fear failing, being rejected, or maybe even telling someone we love them and not hearing that sentiment be returned. Or we doubt: we doubt we will have success in the near future or that someone will love us as much as we love them.

But if we can clear those fears and doubts from within ourselves, then we can gain true self-confidence. Fortunately, we can do that by definitively answering two simple questions. Just two simple questions! Let me share them.

Who am I?

The first question is "Who am I?" That may sound odd, but have you ever run into the following situation? You wake up in the morning and you go to work. You work hard throughout the day. You seem busy with so many things! At the end of the day, you go home late. You feel tired. Even worse, you start to feel empty — you have an emptiness in your mind, a feeling you can't explain. You don't want to do anything next. You find it hard to sleep even though your body is exhausted. Does that sound familiar?

Usually, we are like a machine: we turn on in the morning and we turn off in the evening. And we keep doing things just because the engine is turned on. We are so busy doing things that we don't stop to think and ask ourselves important questions like "Who am I?" and "What is the purpose of my life?" and "Why was I born into this life?"

The fact is that if we don't ask, we will never have the answer. And if we don't know who we are and we don't know what our mission in this life is, it's like we are steering a boat without knowing our destination. Sooner or later, we will wind up floating without any direction — we just float, not getting anywhere. We don't have direction for our lives. And that is why we feel an emptiness when we're back home after having worked hard all day.

Should our lives be that way? Should our minds be so empty?

Let's go with another perspective for a moment. Do you recall a time that you were busy but also happy? When you were exhausted but at the same time fulfilled? Maybe you were doing a charity project together with co-workers on a Saturday. You got back home late, exhausted. But you were happy! That was because you were doing something meaningful.

I believe that if you can gain a clear picture of who you are and what your life's purpose is, then you will know where you are heading. You will have less fear because you will (mostly) know what the challenges will be as you head toward your destination. You will have fewer doubts because you will be aware of what you are doing and why you are doing it. From there, you will earn your confidence from the inside out. Seriously, ask yourself this question: "Who am I?"

What are my strengths?

The next question I would suggest you ask yourself is "What are my strengths?" I learned somewhere that we only use 10% of our brain's capacity. Therefore, we still have 90% of our brains just sitting there, ignored. We have quite a lot potential brainpower waiting to be unleashed! But remember one thing: you cannot be good at everything. We all have our strengths and weaknesses. In fact, we can't have strengths *without* having any weaknesses. But we all have our strengths, too. What are yours? Have you asked yourself that question? I urge you to do that. To learn how you can figure out what your strengths are, check out a book called *Strengths Finder 2.0*.

We usually try to imitate the strengths of the people we admire. For example, fans of the singer Quang Dung have a tendency to imitate his voice as best they can. Fans of Bao Quoc, the comedic actor, tend to imitate his way of acting. Yet we are who we are — we can't be Quang Dung or Bao Quoc, because we are ourselves. If we know exactly what our talents are, then we can focus on maximizing our own unique talents and being ourselves instead of trying to be someone else, which is neither realistic nor effective.

It is natural (and easy) for us to focus on our strengths and leverage them. That is the best way to maximize our value to ourselves and others. So if you haven't asked yourself, "What are my strengths?" then I urge you to ask that question. Once you have the answer, you will know what falls into your strength zone, which is to say what you do best versus what you probably do not do well. If you are aware of both your strengths and weaknesses, you won't be fearful or doubtful in whatever you do. That in turn means you will gain confidence in whatever you do.

Conclusion

You can't gain self-confidence from anyone else or any external sources — you have to gain it from inside yourself. By asking the two questions "Who am I?" and "What are my strengths?" you can start the journey to understanding more about yourself as a person and then become confident from within. That is the strongest kind of confidence you can attain.

Where to seek happiness

I wrote this post on the first day of the Lunar New Year in 2017. The spring sunlight was brightening just a little bit, accompanied by a slight chill, and I had seen lots of New Year's wishes on Facebook.

New Year's wishes are always about happiness, which makes sense seeing as happiness is the critical and ultimate purpose of anyone's life. People usually say that happiness is a journey, a lifetime journey. Yes, I agree! I'm a Buddhist, and for me, happiness goes beyond the window of just one life. My happiness journey will go through a seemingly infinite number of lives. It will be a very long journey until I get there!

What is happiness, anyway? For me, happiness is having a calm and quiet mind and maintaining an inner peace. That way, I can maintain tranquility inside of myself even though this world can sometimes give me way too many challenges and difficulties. Sounds simple, doesn't it? Yet to reach to that level of inner peace and balance requires a long-term journey full of patience, a journey that happens within our mind, a spiritual journey of our own.

On my journey of researching Buddhism and practicing meditation, I have learned many lessons, and what I have learned and experienced thus far has been wonderful! I can see the positive changes happening right inside of my own mind: changing to become simpler, changing to become more peaceful, changing to become happier.

"If we can change the way we see things, we can change the quality of our life. And that's something I can attain through meditation." I learned this teaching from monk **Mathieu Ricard** a while ago when I was reading his book.

The happiness I am talking about is real. I am now more confident in living my life because I now better understand the meaning of my life and I understand what is happening to me on a deeper level. Like the teaching from **Sayadaw U Jotika** says, *"Life is a school, a school that doesn't have a graduation day."*

Life consists of lessons continuously followed by more lessons. Your responsibility is to accept and seriously learn from those lessons. If you haven't finished a lesson, you will need to continue learning it; in one way or another, in one form or another, it will keep coming back so that you can learn it. When you have finished a lesson, the next lesson will always be waiting.

And we don't have to necessarily label things as "good" or "bad," "lucky" or "unlucky," "happy" or "terrible." The more important thing to do is to learn what we can from those experiences and see them as valuable lessons. Once we finish one lesson, we can grow up a little more and gain a little more peace.

In order to best learn life's never-ending lessons, you need to prepare to have and practice having a big, wide-open heart so that you can understand and accept whatever is happening to you and the people around you. From there, you can be flexible and can change your mindset and adapt to the laws of nature, like the fact that people are born, get old, and die. Our lives are full of unexpected events! Whether you accept them or deny them, unexpected things happen.

While we can't change the laws of nature, we *can* learn how to change our thoughts and our reactions to those laws of nature. That lets us see things and phenomena in more suitable ways that obey the laws of nature. Only then can we start to see ourselves and our situations more clearly regardless of how many difficulties, challenges, and unexpected events keep coming into our lives.

Happiness is built on a foundation of compassion, love, and a big, wide-open heart. It's also built upon our every thought, action, and statement, whether they are positive or not. That's where meditation comes into the picture. Meditation is a means to help us sharpen our observational skills, our senses and perceptions, and our ability to see, feel, and learn from what is happening around us. Meditation is an invaluable tool I have learned to use in my life. Now meditation is a critical part of my happiness journey; it's how I move myself toward happiness each day.

Are you pursuing happiness? I am certain that you are. Let your mind relax and be at peace if you haven't already done so. *Then* you will find your true happiness. It is waiting for you right at this present moment!

The barrier to happiness...

"We are more interested in making others believe we are happy than in trying to be happy ourselves." - **Francois de La Rochefoucauld**

It's only when we are able to drop the act of pretending to be happy, when we drop the wish to prove ourselves to others, that our lives become brighter. It's only when we start being our true selves and living our own lives and seeking our own happiness that our lives become brighter. And when that happens, the brightness guides us to our true happiness.

Accumulating peace

"Every moment of peace has a tremendous effect on the mind. Peace of mind, no matter how momentarily, is of great value." — **Sayadaw U Jotika** from ***A Map of the Journey***

How true! And it is even more wonderful when you can grant those momentarily peaceful moments to yourself on a daily basis. As Sayadaw U Jotika teaches, every peaceful moment — even very brief ones — can have an enormous impact on waking up your spiritual potential, your positivity, and that's invaluable.

You don't need to go anywhere in order to attain peaceful moments for yourself. All you need to have is a quiet place where you can sit down and then use the guided script in the QR code below to regularly let your mind and body relax for ten minutes each day.

https://viethungnguyen.com/2019/01/15/hay-thu-gian-lets-relax/

Gradually, you will attain more and more of those brief-but-invaluable moments, peaceful moments that can change you in the most positive ways. And if you keep having more and more of those calm moments, you will accumulate more and more peace within your mind. Just begin by sitting and relaxing your body and mind. Then you'll see the positive changes for yourself!

The wheel of life

Many times, it seems like our life keeps repeating itself the same way every day, based upon our behaviors and customs that we've built up over years. I would call that inertia. What if the inertia that's currently driving our thoughts, actions, and statements each day is not a positive one? Then it can drive our life in a controlling, negative manner. Are you being driven by that kind of inertia? If you are, pause for a while and think thoroughly about your situation. If you let negative inertia continue, you will have more suffering in your life.

In order to make sure you have positive inertia in your life, cultivate positive thoughts, actions, and statements. By doing that, gradually, you will purify your body and mind, until you reach the point that your mindfulness is strong enough to tell you if each of your thoughts, actions, and statements is beneficial to your life or not. Then you can actively take control of your life for the better. No one can do that for you — you have to do it yourself, for the sake of your own life and happiness. Then, your fate can be brighter!

Tears of happiness

When I wrote this blog post, the Lunar New Year of 2018 was just around the corner. Another year was coming! And I no longer get nervous when I'm awaiting special occasions like New Year's and birthdays; in a way, I don't perceive them as "special moments." I know that sounds very dull, but it's really not. Instead, I've been enjoying each and every new day as though it's the first day of the new year or it's my birthday. I am reborn into the world again each day! I still can join others in feeling eager for New Year's Eve. I still enjoy NYE, but I don't miss the NYE excitement once it starts to fade away or after I've grown one year older. I just simply enjoy each moment in a peaceful manner.

On my birthday this year, my nine-year-old daughter told me, "I hope all of your bad days turn into good ones. Be happy all the time!"

That probably sounds like a kid's wish rather than something that could actually happen. Yet I know that my daughter's wish for me truly *is* becoming true! Step by step, I'm attaining the happiness of **#beHATT** (be happy all the time). #beHATT goes beyond the concept of happiness vs. suffering, winning vs. losing. My daughter's wish is perfect! Yes, she said it in an innocent way, but hers is a feasible wish for all of us: be happy all the time!

Just remember that we can only achieve #beHATT once we get beyond the concept of happiness vs. suffering. We can learn a lot from what happens to us without necessarily labeling whatever that is as causing happiness or suffering, joy or sadness, love or hate.

My 41st birthday marked a special milestone in my life: after a few years of preparation, I officially resigned from the position of managing director at KMS Technology Vietnam, the company I co-founded. I did that because I wanted to focus on pursuing my spiritual development journey. During the last nine years that I worked for KMS in the role of co-founder and leader of the company, I contributed to building, developing, and growing the company from zero to nearly 1,000 people.

As you can imagine, people had gotten used to seeing me as a formal and serious leader of the company. But when tears started sliding down my face as I was standing on the stage during the company's year-end party, people saw a different version of me. And some of them didn't prefer that image.

With my mind filled with so many great memories of the company's ups and downs over nine years, I couldn't help being so moved at that moment. I knew that the next day would be different since I wouldn't be spending time with my beloved colleagues. Although I felt very confident about embarking upon my next journey (which I believed would also positively impact many of the people I cared about), the feeling of cohesiveness with my staff naturally turned into tears, tears of happiness.

My very first day after withdrawing from my position was also the first day of a meditation retreat I had been lucky to help organize. We had around 45 meditators who aged between 30 and 70. After four days spent continuously meditating, I delivered a short final speech to end the retreat. Again, I couldn't stop myself from tearing up. And again, they were tears of happiness, this time because I had seen that people had spent four meaningful days being refreshed with so much positive energy that they were ready to go back into a world full of challenges. They were going back feeling refreshed and with more positivity and more wholesome energy.

Once you sit down, close your eyes, and calm your mind, there is no difference between being a Prime Minister or a civilian or being a CEO or a staff member or being rich or poor. There is no difference between being a person full of happiness or a person burdened with too much suffering. Things suddenly become equal.

From that perspective, life is fair. Differences vanish because your mind is now looking inward, not outward. You are looking into yourself rather than looking outside of yourself and comparing yourself with others. We need to look inside in order to really unearth and grow our spiritual potential so that our lives can become more meaningful and we can become happier in this world.

After four days of the retreat, once happiness had overwhelmed us, it was also time for us to say goodbye.

Seeing and feeling the happiness that everyone had attained gave me those tears of joyfulness. And just like what happened during the year-end company gathering at KMS, some people at the retreat told me that they were surprised to see me with tears.

This time, though, I had a very different feeling about hearing that; this time, I was happier, because I knew I could be myself and express my emotions without having to worry about how I looked in the eyes of others. I'm just a regular person with all kinds of emotions, from joyfulness to anger to desire.

Nowadays, I don't have to create a mask for myself. I can cry out of happiness. I have become stronger because I know what happiness can bring to me and how it can change me, inside and out.

Happiness starts with its definition

After I polled readers with the question of "What would make you happy?" I received quite a few answers. It was very exciting to read them all! One person in their 20s responded with the following:

"Be, just be... Be myself, be a part of this universe... Just be, nothing more, nothing less... Then I can experience everything that life has to offer."

That's wonderful! Do you have your own answer? If you do, fill in the form by scanning the QR code below as a commitment to finding your own happiness.

Or maybe you don't have an answer yet. As you think about it, remember:
- There is no "right" or "wrong" answer to this question. The answer is for you to experience yourself as you reach for your own happiness.
- If you don't yet have an answer, start searching for one! Take the first steps on your happiness journey.
- Being able to articulate the answer to this question is a really great step to committing to

living up to the values you think would bring you happiness.
- The answer should act as direction and guidance for your life. And it should be specific and realistic enough to let you validate it in your daily life. If your answer doesn't meet those requirements, then happiness will remain quite vague to you. Seek a more defined answer.
- Everything changes all the time, including the answer to this question; that too will change over time depending on your life experiences and your spiritual maturity. It will be very interesting to see how your answer changes and evolves!
- Often, once we've achieved what we thought would make us happy, most of us realize that that achievement actually isn't bringing us real happiness. That means we need to revise our answer and resume the validation process. It's a wonderful journey of learning about and continuing to develop yourself!

So I'll ask again: What would make you happy?

Necessary space for the mind

I learned a great concept from **Shunmyo Masuno**'s book. Here, I've translated it from Vietnamese into English:

"Whenever you have free space in the house, do you immediately think about how to fill it with things? Because free space means you have more space for things.

Maybe you have an empty table. Really, you only need to put a vase containing a single flower on the table. If you think about also putting magazines, newspapers, books, or candy on the table, it's better to skip that thought. If you always try to fill every empty space, you make your house messier. And if you live in a messy space, one day your mind will also be messy.

Those empty spaces are not for being filled! They exist to help your mind be more relaxed."

This is applicable to all situations in life: arranging your house, handling your daily tasks, organizing your thoughts, etc. We have stuffed too many burdens into our lives for too long. We need to tidy up and remove unnecessary things! And even before doing that, we need to be determined to *not* put more "trash" into our minds and lives.

Filling up space in our mind just to cover any emptiness is not a good idea — that's just running away and hiding. If you find space in your busy mind, instead of filling it up with coffee, cigarettes, alcohol, or even friends, find a quiet place and start to relax your body and mind. If you actively let your mind and body rest, you will feel the enormous positive impact that comes from filling those empty spaces in your mind with peaceful moments.

To a peaceful 2019!

I just had a very busy week, one that was busy with too much joyfulness. I'm tired, yet my mind is very relaxed and peaceful, calmly ready to start 2019.

Last week, I was lucky to be able to attend a five-day meditation retreat under the guidance of my master. The retreat ended on the first day of 2019.

During the last night of the year, while many people were busy noisily celebrating and entertaining themselves, our group of about 40 people was celebrating New Year's Eve in silence by going to bed early in order to wake up around 4 a.m. the next day, just in time for the routine daily start of the retreat.

I headed the team that organized the retreat, and during the last night of the retreat, my heart was jumping quite a bit. The retreat had gone smoothly. People had been meditating well. Tranquility, relaxation, and happiness had started appearing on the faces of the meditators, including mine. Peace and quiet were very much present within my body and mind on that last night of the year.

What was even more special was that: time wasn't having much of an impact on me. During the last night of the year, my wife and I were both sitting in quietness. (Although we were in different areas because female and male areas were separated.) Our little daughter was not with us that night, but our minds were so still that we didn't miss her too much. And surprisingly, I didn't feel like I needed to celebrate the new year. I was only aware of the simplicity and peacefulness that were suffusing my mind after I had spent a few days continuously meditating. That was a wonderful experience!

Happiness can't be found externally — it can only be found inside of our own mind, whenever and wherever we are. I think many of us know and understand that, yet many of us haven't directly experienced a feeling of real inner peace. I was so moved and so happy to have gotten a few moments full of quietness and happiness!

Midnight came. Bursting sounds of fireworks came from far away, booming at the other end of the city. But my mind was strangely quiet.

When a new year arrives, we usually wish everyone health and good fortune. We usually set our next objectives and goals and our ambitious plans for the year to come. And we pray, too — we pray hard for good things to come to our lives and our families.

This year, beside praying, I and the others in our retreat group had equipped ourselves with very powerful tools to use in the new year: mindfulness and self-awareness. Mindfulness is the most powerful tool that helps to bring ourselves the best things in life, I believe. And so we were ready for the new year, ready in a mindful and peaceful manner.

When peace comes from within, we can be simpler, more open-minded, and more independent. We can care more for ourselves and for our own lives as well as for the people around us. That's the foundation of happiness.

I'm a meditator, and given what I have experienced through meditation and all of the benefits meditation has brought into my life thus far, I will never stop promoting meditation and mindful living. People who are very mindful don't harm anyone, including themselves, and that's the root of happiness. I started 2019 in quietness and peace. How about you?

"May peace come to everyone. May everyone have no suffering. May everyone have no sickness." That's what we prayed during our metta meditation at 8 a.m. on the first day of 2019. My master guided us through the prayer. That simple-yet-moving, powerful, compassionate prayer came from each one of us, from each of our peaceful hearts on New Year's Eve. A meaningful, full-of-love way to start a new year.

Peace can only come to those who are able to maintain positive thoughts, actions, and statements. If you want to attain that kind of peacefulness, start learning and practicing mindfulness. And especially meditate!

Most of us fail in our search for happiness...but we can succeed

Happiness starts with having good self-esteem and being responsible for our actions, our statements, and our thoughts. Only then can we take care of ourselves without being harmful to anyone, including ourselves. "You can only rise as high as your self-esteem," says **Sayadaw U Jotika** in the book *A Map of the Journey*. This teaching is simple, yet deep and powerful.

My meditation master once delivered a short talk at KMS Technology Vietnam. He started with his own story. He is a monk who practices the Theravada Buddhism tradition, and his robes are quite different from the popular Buddhist monk robes in Vietnam. When asked why he became ordained and followed the path of Buddha, he told us that his answer was and still is very simple: just like everyone else, he's seeking happiness. And the path he has been pursuing is the path he has found to be suitable for himself. That same path may not be suitable for others. As time has passed, he has confirmed that yes, it's the right path for him on his way to find truth.

He continued, "Though everyone seeks happiness, most of us fail." Usually, even during our last few moments before we depart from this world, we are still seeking happiness because we still haven't found it yet. That is reflected in our last wishes or the likes. Once you do have true happiness in your body and mind, you no longer seek it, he pointed out.

I was shocked by his conclusion that most of us fail in our pursuit of happiness. Could that be true? Unfortunately, yes, that scenario is far too common.

We are born into this world, we grow up in this world, and ultimately, we depart from this world. We keep searching for happiness throughout our entire lives, and most of us fail. So is there a different way to search for happiness?

I think there is. I believe that there *is* an answer to this challenge. I believe that because I have carefully observed the life of my master and the life of my master's teacher. They are proof that we can have a meaningful life without spending it forever searching. That doesn't mean they are separate from this world or that they are "dry" and without compassion and love. Anyone who has the chance to meet my teacher or his teacher would certainly feel their infinite kindness and compassion and would recognize that these men are simple, intimate, and respectful people. Above of all, they are full of wisdom and insightful teachings. They share and instruct from their hearts. I'm so lucky to be their student.

The other reason why I think there's a different way to find happiness comes from my own experiences over the past five years of meditating. I know now that I can find the hidden parts of myself I didn't know about before. I can live for my own self and I can be my own self. I can be more refreshed each day, more positive each day, more energetic each day, and more confident each day.

I believe that I deserve happiness. And in order to deserve that, I have to be patient and practice mindfulness each and every day.

Preparing for our next life

Question: *Do we need to prepare for our next life?*

Answer: This depends on whether you believe there is a next life or not and also on your understanding of that life. More importantly, though, how do we to prepare for our next life?

I believe in reincarnation and that I will have at least one more life to live after the current one. Therefore, for me the answer is yes, I do need to prepare for my next life right now so that I can transition to the next one smoothly once it's time for that to happen.

Eyes close, and then eyes open again soon. One door closes; then you open another one. Which door you choose very much depends on your beliefs. And how you prepare to choose is certainly derived from what you think, do, and say in the present moment.

So the answer is simple… yet you need a lot of faith, patience, persistence, and determination to attain the right result.

A quiet lake

"We can make our minds so like still water that beings gather about us that they may see, it may be, their own images, and so live for a moment with a clearer, perhaps even with a fiercer life because of our quiet." — **William Butler Yeats**

I agree very much with what Yeats says! We should be a still and quiet lake in our minds. Firstly, we do that for ourselves. Then, once we have enough stillness in our mind, people around us will see themselves reflected in that mirror of peace, a mirror that is also full of love and wisdom.

It's not complicated to live that life once we're in it, but it is hard to make it happen. However, to live a life full of meaning and peace is worth every ounce of effort it takes!

Hell and freedom

I learned a valuable lesson from monk *Ajahn Brahm* that goes like this: *"Whenever you don't like being where you are, then you are in prison. A prison of your mind. You don't have to physically be in prison to be imprisoned."* If we're not wise enough, many times we are imprisoned by our own mind.

If you can deeply connect with this concept, you will see that it gives you a lot of freedom, namely the freedom to work with your mind to liberate yourself from the prison of your own mind, to liberate yourself from your lack of knowledge.

Certainly, escaping from "prison" is never going to be easy. But with the right attitude and a strong desire and intention to be free, you can secure your freedom and liberate yourself within your own mind. And the way to begin gaining that freedom is to understand more about your mind.

Freedom lies directly ahead

Many different roads lie ahead of us. You need to choose for yourself the one you would like to follow. That's a basic right and a basic freedom for all of us. However, many times we are so confused and unclear about what lies ahead that we only see the obvious road and we overlook less obvious but more beautiful roads. Or even worse, sometimes we choose to follow a dead-end road that we don't realize is a dead-end road. As a result, we keep wasting our time and health.

Be mindful and be self-aware. Choose your road carefully! That's the key to true happiness.

Beautiful moments

A beautiful life is not in the past and not in the future: it can only happen right here and right now. Beautiful moments are brief; they disappear quickly and often never return. Therefore, you need to be utterly and completely in the present in order to enjoy those beautiful moments. Otherwise, you will miss them!

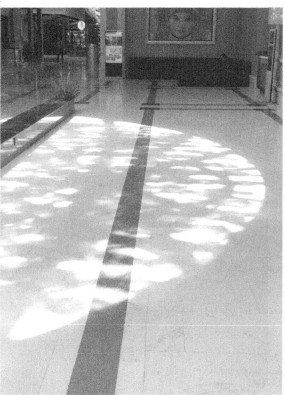

The barrier of detachment

During an inspirational talk I gave about leadership to a group of key leaders at a software company, I got the following question from the audience: "During the course of your personal development, after you left your position and work responsibilities behind, what is the biggest barrier you have been faced with?"

Leaving a position and its accompanying responsibilities is a big challenge for all of us, I think. We usually have to take charge of many responsibilities throughout our lives: the responsibilities of being a son, being a husband, being a father; the responsibilities that come along with our ambitions; the responsibilities that are a result of us wanting to maintain good appearances in front of others, etc. We have thousands of reasons to advocate what we're doing and what we believe in. Only time that can tell whether what we're doing is right or wrong.

Do we often ask ourselves if what we're doing is appropriate, necessary, and beneficial for our lives? If what we're doing is helping us gain more wisdom and gradually helping us become more knowledgeable, more mature, and happier?

It's hard to answer "yes" or "no" to that. I think the best way to answer that question is to use your present understanding and wisdom to come up with the best possible course of action for what you need to do. As long as your actions are steering you toward being more mature, wiser, and happier, those actions are worth doing. Step by step, you can map out how to accomplish what you think you need to achieve.

During this process, you need to continuously, closely, and objectively observe and feel what impact your actions are having on your body and mind. Do you feel more positive or negative each day? More open-minded or close-minded? Does life seem simpler or more complicated? Are you more independent of or dependent on your external conditions and the people around you? Are you more compassionate or aloof? More peaceful or chaotic? Directly observing your body and mind can help you determine if what you're doing is reasonable, correct, and meaningful for your life. And whenever you realize you need to make adjustments or changes to improve your life, you become more mature and gain more happiness. You live a more meaningful life, a more noble life, a happier life each day.

The road to inner peace and happiness needs to include more simplicity, openness, independence, and compassion. And simplicity includes detachment. That said, making this concept of "detachment" happen is not an easy job at all. What do we need to detach or drop? Should we just drop everything immediately? No, it's not that simple.

The question I received that day centers on concerns about being detached. That's a challenging question for anyone! Here are my thoughts regarding detachment.

You can only drop something once you're ready for that detachment. Many people seemed to very much respect my decision to withdraw from my managing director position at KMS Technology Vietnam once things were going well. People usually think that it must be an enormous sacrifice for anyone who is in similar situation to do that — after all, I was at the top of an organization of nearly 1,000 employees that is a leading company in Vietnam's software services industry. But for me, the truth is that leaving my position happened very naturally, like a soft, quick breeze going by my face. I didn't have to struggle much internally to make that decision. I had felt and known that I needed to walk away from my business life a long time ago — I just needed time to thoroughly prepare for that withdrawal and to do it at the right time. I realized that my definition of happiness and success doesn't include attaining top positions. That is not where my true happiness lies, I don't think.

If you don't see happiness at the end of the road you're on, then leaving that road is quite inevitable and easy. I think seeing and knowing what you need to detach from is the first part of "drop it" process. And that's the easier part. The more difficult part is persisting through the preparations and making it happen eventually. It only happens if you really want it. And going through the necessary preparations requires a lot of faith, persistence, effort, patience, and determination, plus of course you need time (sometimes a lot of time!) to finish the preparation phase. For me, that phase lasted around five years once I knew I needed to withdraw from the business world. And now I'm here, becoming an author and a speaker while continuing to work on my happiness pursuit.

Once you have experienced life's challenges and difficulties and learned from them, it becomes easier to drop things and live a simpler life. You *can* detach yourself from responsibilities and burdens! I have read a book called **Goodbye, Things: The New Japanese Minimalism**. It is about cleaning up your house. From reading it, I learned that "Throwing away your things is not just simply throwing everything you have," as the author says. It's more about asking yourself, "Which things are important and essential for my life?" Then, only keep those things! Find ways to drop the rest. This enables you to remove a lot of things that are not important and not essential to your life — in other words, those countless unnecessary things that keep adding burdens. Once you've dropped them, your life will become simpler and more peaceful. More importantly, your life will become brighter. This entire process will function like a "purifier" for your life.

What is important to you, to your own life, to your own happiness? Once you can answer that question thoroughly and deeply, you can detach from a lot more in this world. Gaining more wisdom is just as important as gaining a greater ability to detach, I think.

But! It's important to note that although we should prepare ourselves to detach from unnecessary things, especially external things, we should *never* drop our personal responsibility to pursue our own happiness and our own life. The good news is that dropping our unnecessary burdens will make us even more ready to search for our true happiness!

"The myth is stronger than the truth..."

I heard these meaningful lyrics on my way to an appointment one morning:

"The myth is stronger than the truth, and the truth can sometimes lie
To see it all for what it was, you need an uncorrupted eye
Was the journey worth it? Only time will tell."
— ***The Beat Hotel | Allan Taylor***

It's true — we are usually overwhelmed by myths, because they often seem much stronger and bigger than the truth. And fear often comes from myths, from the unknown. Most of the time, though, that fear isn't founded on anything real.

We all sometimes fall into this trap. Fear comes from what we don't know, from truths we don't see. And because we keep on not knowing, fear keeps haunting us and building up more and more fear in us. Paradoxically, we're kind of addicted to this mysterious not-knowing, to being in this trap. Can we break this loop? How?

More importantly, do you see the loop? Do you want to break it? I can't answer that question for you. You have to answer it for yourself, for *your* life, for *your* happiness.

And then, even once we think we know the truth, sometimes it's a lie. That's because we came to know the wrong truth. Seeing the real truth is something we have to continuously strive for; we have to continuously sharpen our observation skills as we live our lives.

It's often hard for us to see the real truth right away. But as we mature, we can see deeper and deeper layers of truth.

The ability to see the truth is embedded within the practice of meditation. In a nutshell, meditation is all about sharpening your observation skills and your knowing of your body and mind within the present moment, which after all is the only moment we can truly live in. Past and future are all just illusions and thoughts. We don't live there — we live in the here and now. But our minds keep trying to convince us to live in the past or the future, and that's how we miss seeing the truth big-time.

Being mindful, living in the present, and knowing what is happening in the present gives us an "uncorrupted eye" and helps us see things with greater clarity.

Many times, we don't want to believe in what we see or we may just skip seeing what we need to see. Only time and our courage to learn and experience life can tell what is good for us and what is not. We need to see the truth, not skip over it.

The marks waves leave

Waves always come to the shore and then return to the ocean. Although the waves are only on the beach for a very brief moment, it's enough time for them to leave beautiful traces behind. The marks waves leave…

Like those waves, we come into this world and then depart from it. Even if we live for 100 years, when we look back, those 100 years are just like a breeze passing by us on the beach, flowing through the air - the way waves flow onto and off of the sand. What do we leave behind in this world? What are our life's marks?

Many people have a burning wish in their heart to leave their mark in the world. If they're not careful, that ambition could become an intense fire, burning themselves, burning their lives, and burning their loved ones. We have to watch out for this!

So what *can* we leave behind? I think we don't really have to worry about our legacies, frankly. That's because with each of our thoughts, actions, and statements, we have cultivated the soil of our lives. And like the waves, we leave many traces behind throughout our lives, whether that is intentional or not.

Rather than concerning ourselves with our legacies, the most important thing we need to do is to be in the here and now: we need to continuously and mindfully observe our thoughts, actions, and statements. We need to observe them in order to understand how they impact our life and mind. And whenever we become aware of harmful thoughts, actions, or statements, we need to stop them. Then we can replace them with positive thoughts, actions, and statements that help us live more meaningful lives, more beautiful lives, *happier* lives.

Our responsibility is to keep cultivating peaceful and positive thoughts, actions, and statements. Then, gradually, the fruits of happiness will come into our lives. And we need to continuously observe and make self-adjustments, just like the waves flow out of and into the ocean nonstop. We must continuously observe. We must continuously adjust.

If we do that, we don't need to pay attention to what "marks" we leave behind. In accordance with the laws of nature, the "seeds" of peace and happiness will automatically create and leave behind positive "marks," that is, a positive legacy.

The key to achieving this is not to put too much emphasis on what we want to leave behind. Everything comes and goes — waves, clouds, breezes. Doing everything you can to cultivate positivity in the here and now means you will leave behind a big blue sky, wide open and full of sunlight for the world to enjoy.

We leave in order to return. We're just like those waves that keep coming and going. Those waves never pay attention to what they create on the beach, yet they leave behind such beautiful traces, naturally and peacefully. If we keep cultivating peaceful "seeds" of actions, statements, and thoughts, our lives will be like those waves and we will likewise leave behind beautiful and meaningful traces. And we can also live a more intense, more meaningful life each day.

The Happiness Journal

THE LAST FEW WORDS

I hope you have enjoyed the thoughts I've shared in this book and have been able to relive many happy and meaningful moments along with me.

I wrote and published these articles on my website mostly for me, with the simple intention of describing my feelings during various times of my life. I've kept jotting down my thoughts and the happy and meaningful moments that have happened to me over the past ten years.

At the end of July 2019, I had a chance to visit a beach resort owned by one of my friends. We had dinner at night, right on the Cam Ranh beach, which is a beautiful and peaceful bay next to the city of Nha Trang. The two of us enjoyed our food and sipped bottles of beer, watching the big, round, beautiful moon gradually emerge from behind a dark cloud in the sky. It was so beautiful and peaceful!

During the course of our conversation, I learned that my advice and thoughts had helped my friend achieve his current accomplishments, including his new-found financial independence. (You could say he had become financially worry-free.) That independence gave him the freedom to use his time doing whatever he loves to do, to be himself and to have the kind of life he wants. Hearing that I had been able to influence him in such a positive way made me so happy! I was thrilled to know that I could be so useful and could provide such an impact for someone.

That was the moment that I decided that I needed to figure out how to reach and help more people. I had already been writing my blog for a while and had posted lots of articles, and within six weeks, I had compiled the posts, edited them, and made them into a book. And then I released that book (in Vietnamese) in mid-November 2019. This book is the English version of my original book. It's not a complete translation of the Vietnamese version, however — while I kept much of the content and translated it into English, I did omit a few articles that might not have been relevant for English-speaking audiences, plus I added a few more articles to the English version. I've been able to take charge of the entire self-publishing process for this book and have made it available in both paperback and Kindle format.

Being able to live our own lives, be our own selves, and be honest with ourselves is quite a big challenge for anyone, I think. But once we *can* do those things, an invaluable gift awaits us: ***happiness***.

I believe that only people who have an in-depth understanding of the laws of nature that govern our bodies and minds and who respect and follow those laws of nature will have fulfilled and happy lives. Having a happy life doesn't mean that every moment is full of joy — even a happy life includes many challenges and burdens and dissatisfactions. But I believe that once you can be your true self, you will have more and more happy, positive moments each day no matter what challenges arise.

We do not find happiness by running away from suffering or by covering up our suffering — we're happy because we have deeply learned every lesson that has been thrown at us in the form of challenges and difficulties. We become more mature and can accept reality as it is. That's when we can choose the best response to what is happening to us and act in the most positive and beneficial way.

We can only live in the present moment, right here and right now. The past and the future are purely thoughts and figments of our imagination. While we can't change the past, we should be confident that we can greatly influence our futures. We can do that by cultivating positive thoughts, actions, and statements in the present moment. That is true freedom: the freedom to respond to whatever is happening to us in a positive, beneficial manner. Those present-moment thoughts, actions, and statements can heal the wounds of the past as well as plant seeds of future happiness in your life, seeds that become fruits of happiness later on. That's the ultimate freedom. Yet this freedom it is also our personal responsibility — we are responsible for grabbing the opportunities that occur in each of our present moments to know where we're heading, to make necessary changes if needed, and to go beyond ourselves. All of this allows us to reach our destination of peace and happiness.

What would make you happy? Who do you want to be in the next year? In the next three years, five years, 20 years, and once you're 80? Seriously consider your answers to those questions. Deeply knowing your answers can guide you closer to happiness.

But wait! Before you put down this book, as a self-published author, I ask for your help — could you leave feedback and a review? And if you think this book has been and will be helpful in your pursuit of happiness, it would be helpful for others. You can help more readers find out about my book by leaving your feedback or rating at: https://www.amazon.com/dp/B07XRB7CV4 or scanning the QR code below.

Many thanks for your help! May all great things and peace be with you.

About the author

After graduating in 1999 from Polytechnics University of Ho Chi Minh City, Vietnam, Viet Hung started his career as a software application programmer. He then worked his way through various positions: he was a software business analyst, project manager, engineering manager, and director. From 2001 to 2006, he went back and forth to work in the US.

In late 2008, he co-founded KMS Technology, offering software development services to software companies in US. As the managing director of KMS Technology Vietnam, he grew the company from zero to 1,000 people by 2018. Under his leadership, KMS Technology Vietnam became the preeminent software development services company in the industry.

Early in 2018, he decided to resign from his position at KMS Technology Vietnam and continue his journey of his pursuit of happiness. He currently lives in Saigon, Vietnam, with his lovely wife and daughter.

He shares his thoughts on his personal website: www.viethungnguyen.com. You can reach him via email at: me@viethungnguyen.com.

V1.9.4.

Made in the USA
Coppell, TX
07 August 2021